The Laws That Protect

Youth with Special Needs

LIVING WITH A SPECIAL NEED

Attention-Deficit/Hyperactivity Disorder

Autism

Blindness and Vision Impairment

Brain Injury

Chronic Illness

Deaf and Hard of Hearing

Emotional Disturbance

Gender Issues

Intellectual Disabilities

Learning Disabilities

Physical Challenges

Protective Services

Speech Impairment

The Foster Care System

The Juvenile Court System

The Laws That Protect Youth with Special Needs

LIVING WITH A SPECIAL NEED

The Laws That Protect Youth with Special Needs

JOAN ESHERICK

MASON CREST

Mason Crest
450 Parkway Drive, Suite D
Broomall, PA 19008
www.masoncrest.com

Printed and bound in the United States of America.

Series ISBN: 978-1-4222-3027-5
ISBN: 978-1-4222-3039-8
ebook ISBN: 978-1-4222-8824-5

Library of Congress Cataloging-in-Publication Data

Esherick, Joan, author.
  The laws that protect youth with special needs / Joan Esherick.
     pages cm. — (The laws that protect youth with special needs)
  Includes index.
  ISBN 978-1-4222-3039-8 (hardback) — ISBN 978-1-4222-3027-5 (series) — ISBN
978-1-4222-8824-5 (ebook) 1. Youth with disabilities—Legal status, laws, etc.—United
States—Juvenile literature. 2. Discrimination against people with disabilities—Law and
legislation—United States—Juvenile literature. I. Title.
  KF480.E83 2014
  342.7308'772—dc23
                                                          2014010651

Picture credits: Benjamin Stewart: pp. 58, 59, 60, 75, 79, 81, 82; Corbis: pp. 23, 77, 84;
Library of Congress: p. 25; PhotoDisc: pp. 24, 26, 41, 42, 56, 57, 76, 78, 80, 98, 99,
100, 113, 114, 115; Photo Spin: pp. 55, 111; Seeing Eye: p. 116; Susquehanna Service
Dogs: p. 117. U.S. National Archives: p. 26; Individual in the photograph on p. 57 is a
model, and this image is for illustrative purposes only.

CONTENTS

KEY ICONS TO LOOK FOR:

Text-Dependent Questions: These questions send the reader back to the text for more careful attention to the evidence presented there.

Words to Understand: These words with their easy-to-understand definitions will increase the reader's understanding of the text, while building vocabulary skills.

Series Glossary of Key Terms: This back-of-the book glossary contains terminology used throughout this series. Words found here increase the reader's ability to read and comprehend higher-level books and articles in this field.

Research Projects: Readers are pointed toward areas of further inquiry connected to each chapter. Suggestions are provided for projects that encourage deeper research and analysis.

Sidebars: This boxed material within the main text allows readers to build knowledge, gain insights, explore possibilities, and broaden their perspectives by weaving together additional information to provide realistic and holistic perspectives.

A child with special needs is not defined by his disability.
It is just one part of who he is.

INTRODUCTION

Each child is unique and wonderful. And some children have differences we call special needs. Special needs can mean many things. Sometimes children will learn differently, or hear with an aid, or read with Braille. A young person may have a hard time communicating or paying attention. A child can be born with a special need, or acquire it by an accident or through a health condition. Sometimes a child will be developing in a typical manner and then become delayed in that development. But whatever problems a child may have with her learning, emotions, behavior, or physical body, she is always a person first. She is not defined by her disability; instead, the disability is just one part of who she is.

Inclusion means that young people with and without special needs are together in the same settings. They learn together in school; they play together in their communities; they all have the same opportunities to belong. Children learn so much from each other. A child with a hearing impairment, for example, can teach another child a new way to communicate using sign language. Someone else who has a physical disability affecting his legs can show his friends how to play wheelchair basketball. Children with and without special needs can teach each other how to appreciate and celebrate their differences. They can also help each other discover how people are more alike than they are different. Understanding and appreciating how we all have similar needs helps us learn empathy and sensitivity.

In this series, you will read about young people with special needs from the unique perspectives of children and adolescents who are experiencing the disability firsthand. Of course, not all children with a particular disability are the same as the characters in the stories. But the stories demonstrate at an emotional level how a special need impacts a child, his family, and his friends. The factual material in each chapter will expand your horizons by adding to your knowledge about a particular disability. The series as a whole will help you understand differences better and appreciate how they make us all stronger and better.

—*Cindy Croft*
Educational Consultant

YOUTH WITH SPECIAL NEEDS provides a unique forum for demystifying a wide variety of childhood medical and developmental disabilities. Written to captivate an adolescent audience, the books bring to life the challenges and triumphs experienced by children with common chronic conditions such as hearing loss, mental retardation, physical differences, and speech difficulties. The topics are addressed frankly through a blend of fiction and fact. Students and teachers alike can move beyond the information provided by accessing the resources offered at the end of each text.

This series is particularly important today as the number of children with special needs is on the rise. Over the last two decades, advances in pediatric medical techniques have allowed children who have chronic illnesses and disabilities to live longer, more functional lives. As a result, these children represent an increasingly visible part of North American population in all aspects of daily life. Students are exposed to peers with special needs in their classrooms, through extracurricular activities, and in the community. Often, young people have misperceptions and unanswered questions about a child's disabilities—and more important, his or her *abilities*. Many times, there is no vehicle for talking about these complex issues in a comfortable manner.

This series provides basic information that will leave readers with a deeper understanding of each condition, along with an awareness of some of the associated emotional impacts on affected children, their families, and their peers. It will also encourage further conversation about these issues. Most important, the series promotes a greater comfort for its readers as they live, play, and work side by side with these individuals who have medical and developmental differences—youth with special needs.

—*Dr. Lisa Albers, Dr. Carolyn Bridgemohan, Dr. Laurie Glader*
Medical Consultants

Words to Understand

disability: An impairment that substantially affects one or more major life activities.

severe disability: Needing to use a wheelchair, cane, crutches, or walker; having a mental or emotional condition that seriously interferes with everyday activities; having mental retardation; or being unable to perform activities of daily living without help.

assistive technology devices: Equipment that allows people with disabilities to be more independent, including but not limited to computers, communication devices, and word prediction or word recognition software.

dyslexia: A learning disorder that causes someone to see numbers and letters backward or reversed in order.

spina bifida: A birth defect wherein the baby's spine doesn't develop properly in the womb, and that often leads to paralysis.

birth defect: A permanent physical or medical disability that is present at birth.

physical therapy: Special treatment to help a patient improve gross motor skills like walking, sitting, rolling over, climbing, and going up or down steps.

occupational therapy: Special treatment to help a patient improve fine motor skills like holding a pencil, writing, grasping, drawing, keyboarding, and operating a mouse.

speech therapy: Special techniques used to help someone improve their ability to speak and be understood.

prosthetic device: A man-made device used to replace a missing body part.

TTY or TDD: Interchangeable acronyms referring to a device that enables people who are deaf, hard of hearing, or speech-disabled to use the telephone by typing messages instead of talking and listening. TTY stands for "teletypewriter." TDD stands for "telecommunication device for the deaf."

special education: Instruction or teaching strategies designed to meet the unique needs of a child with a disability.

1

DEFINING SPECIAL NEEDS

Imagine sitting in a classroom with thirty-four other students. Look around you. What do you see? You might notice the cute blonde smiling in the corner or the wisecracking guy with the gorgeous brown eyes. Perhaps you're attracted to the muscle-bulging football player in the back row or the shy chess team captain on your left. Maybe you know the Goth kid staring out the window or the cheerleader who just spilled her papers all over the floor. Yes, you see different outward appearances, clothing styles, personalities, and interests. But what you might not see, what may or may not be visible are the special needs represented in the room. Look again.

Statistically, of the thirty-five students in your class,

five (four guys and one girl) struggle to overcome learning
 disabilities,
two have been (or will be) arrested and charged with a crime,
three have asthma or other respiratory conditions,
one has a chronic heart condition or is in poor health,
an estimated four to seven have psychiatric disorders,
nearly three live in the homes of relatives who are not their
 parents,
two have been abused (physically, sexually, or psychologi-
 cally),
two have disabilities or health problems severe enough to
 limit activity,

four require at least part-time specialized educational support,
nearly three get bullied regularly in school,
four of ten girls will get pregnant before they reach age
twenty, and
at least three contemplate (or have contemplated) suicide.

These observations aren't just guesses; the numbers listed here represent validated research statistics provided by organizations like the American Bar Association (ABA), the U.S. Department of Health and Human Services, the U.S. Department of Education, the National Center for Educational Statistics (NCES), and the National Center for Health Statistics (NCHS). Here are more of their findings:

According to the U.S. Department of Education's National Institute on Disability and Rehabilitation Research, one out of five Americans has a diagnosable *disability*. Almost half of these are considered to have a *severe disability*.

The Centers for Disease Control and Prevention's (CDC) National Center for Health Statistics (NCHS) found that in 2008, more than 50 million Americans had a disability of some kind.

The same CDC study reported that eight million Americans used *assistive technology devices* (ATDs) to help them move or walk. Another five million used ATDs to help them see or hear.

Physical disabilities don't represent the only special needs:

The American Bar Association records that there were 1,500,000 juvenile arrests in 2002. That accounts for two percent of the entire juvenile population in the United States, or nearly one out of every fifty kids.

The National Youth Network estimates that nearly one out of ten minors will experience at least one episode of major depression by the time they reach age fifteen.

A 2011 U.S. Department of Health and Human Services study reports that about 400,540 children under eighteen years of age lived with families who were not their parents— they lived in foster care.

The Children's Bureau of the U.S. Department of Health and Human Services records that 879,000 children in the United States were victims of verified neglect, abuse, or other forms of maltreatment in 2002. That's roughly one abused child out of every eighty-five kids. For each of these reported cases, it is estimated that two go unreported.

Physical disabilities, learning disabilities, psychological disorders, juvenile delinquency, foster care, abuse, teen pregnancy—these issues require support and intervention for the people who face them. Your imaginary class represents the diversity and complexity of the issues. While that diversity has its advantages (much can be learned from those who differ from us), it also brings challenges. Along with varying circumstances, family backgrounds, and health statuses, many of these students have special needs.

Special needs come in all shapes and sizes. From the blind student requesting Braille textbooks to the recently adopted international student seeking an English tutor to the teen with heart disease needing homebound instruction while she awaits a transplant— each requires out-of-the-ordinary support and resources to survive and succeed. Though their specifics differ, all have special needs.

Special needs are those things necessary for a person's well-being that differ from the norm. We could say, for example, that all students in America *need* to learn to read. Reading is a skill necessary for well-being in a culture that requires reading in so much of everyday life (traffic signs, street names, mailing addresses, health insurance forms, job applications, food product labels, banking, etc.). All Americans need reading skills to succeed in American culture. The ability to read is a need, but it is not a *special* need. When a child is blind, however, or has **dyslexia**, he can't learn to read the way other children do. His need to read has to be met differently than the norm. That child has a special need.

Many circumstances can cause a person to develop special needs. Sickness, chronic medical conditions, or traumatic injury can result in special needs. Sometimes a person's actions or choices make additional support necessary, as in teen pregnancy, drug addiction, or juvenile delinquency. In other cases, circumstances beyond a person's control create an at-risk environment resulting in the need for special help or intervention (abusive home situations or foster care, for example). Volumes could be written about each special need and its contributing circumstances, but for the purposes of this book, we will group special needs into four categories:

special needs resulting from physical challenges,
special needs resulting from psychiatric and learning disorders,
special needs resulting from behavioral choices, and
special needs resulting from environmental circumstances.

Lindsay's wide smile brightens the darkest of rooms. Her infectious giggle and wry humor make her popular with other students in her class. Seeing Lindsay seated in the art room working on her clay sculpture and bantering with other girls about who likes whom or who made the basketball team, you'd never suspect that Lindsay has special needs—until the bell rings signaling that it's time to go to the next class. Then you'd see Lindsay's "buddy" dash to the corner nearest the door, grab a pair of aluminum crutches with arm supports, and return them to Lindsay. Fitting the forearm cuffs around each lower arm and grabbing the vinyl, contoured handgrips, Lindsay plants each rubber-tipped crutch on the floor and pushes her body upward. Her braced legs follow.

Lindsay can walk only with the aid of crutches. It's been that way for her since she was born with a condition called ***spina bifida***. Like one out of every thousand children in the United States, Lindsay's spine failed to close properly as she developed in her mother's womb, and by the time she was born, her spinal cord was damaged enough to cause paralysis in her legs. Because of this ***birth defect***, Lindsay has physical limitations that cause her to need help with standing, walking, dressing, pulling doors open (while holding onto crutches), navigating steps, and making it to class on time. Lindsay has special needs resulting from physical challenges.

Spina bifida isn't the only condition that can result in physical challenges from birth. Premature birth (when a child is born too early into the pregnancy), genetic disorders, viral infections, substance abuse by the mother while pregnant, problems during birth, the environment, and side effects of medications can all result in lifelong physical challenges.

When Donnie was born he looked like a perfectly healthy baby, except that his umbilical cord had wrapped around his neck and nearly strangled him as he was delivered. Though the pressure on his neck caused his face to turn blue, doctors unwrapped the cord, revived him quickly, and he seemed to be fine. As months passed, however, his parents noticed that Donnie was developing differently than other children. They soon discovered that he had mild cerebral palsy (a brain injury resulting from oxygen deprivation at or near birth that causes problems in motor function). Donnie's brain injury made it impossible for him to move his arms and legs normally. It also slurred his speech. Over the next several years, Donnie required ***physical therapy***, ***occupational therapy***, and ***speech therapy*** to help him learn to walk and talk.

Donnie had special needs resulting from physical challenges caused at birth.

Physical challenges resulting in special needs don't always begin at birth. Twelve-year-old Dawson lost his right foot while cutting the grass when he slipped on a wet incline and the lawn mower he was using rolled over his outstretched leg. He now needs a *prosthetic device* to stand, walk, or run.

Sixteen-year-old Li Ming didn't experience physical challenges until a fire destroyed her home near Christmas in 1998. The searing, smoke-filled air she breathed while trying to escape the flames permanently damaged her lungs. Since the fire, instead of running on the track team (as she used to do), the petite teenager can barely walk without feeling short of breath. To ease her breathing, Li Ming uses a portable oxygen tank, which pumps life-giving air through a clear plastic hose into a specially designed tube she wears in her nose. Li Ming has special needs.

Having special needs resulting from physical challenges often means needing help with walking, talking, eating, breathing, seeing, hearing, reading, writing, communicating with others, or maintaining personal hygiene. This assistance can include, among other things, special appliances (wheelchairs, hearing aids, crutches, prosthetic devices, braces, or walking canes), building modifications (wheelchair ramps, wide doorways, low-placed wall switches, and railings), medical equipment (ventilators, oxygen tanks, insulin pumps, etc.), or communication devices (laptop computers, electronic voice communicators, *TTY* or *TDD* devices). But not all special needs are so complicated.

Some special needs can be as simple as needing more time to finish a task. In Lindsay's case, because she needs more time to get from one class to the next than the allotted time permits, her teachers issued her a permanent hall pass that allows her to arrive late for her classes without penalty. The need for more time to make it to class is one of Lindsay's special needs.

Special needs resulting from physical challenges are the most visible and best understood special needs. It's pretty obvious that if a student is blind she will need books on tape or books written in Braille to succeed in school. If a person uses a wheelchair, he will need a ramp or elevator to go upstairs. However, some special needs are less obvious.

Seventeen-year-old Stephanie seems like an average teenager: she listens to her favorite CDs, enjoys soccer, hangs out with her friends, and looks forward to graduation. Like most students, she likes some of her classes, but detests others. Stephanie does well in certain subjects and poorly in a few. She studies hard but rarely gets grades that reflect her effort. She commiserates with classmates about homework, special projects, long-term assignments, and her teachers' "unfair" grading practices. But most of her classmates don't know how hard it is for Stephanie to learn; this high school senior can barely read.

It's not that Stephanie isn't smart. Intelligence assessments estimate that Stephanie has an IQ of well over 140. This is the Stephanie most of her friends see: the bright student who grasps difficult concepts and talks about them easily. But Stephanie struggles with many basics: reading, spelling, writing, following directions, and discerning left from right—a fact she hides from her peers. Though she excels in mathematics, particularly logic, she can't do a word problem to save her soul, unless someone reads the problem to her. Though strong in class discussion and able to comprehend abstract subjects, she can't write a paper explaining what she understands.

Stephanie has dyslexia, a condition described by the International Dyslexia Association as a language-based learning disability. This disorder is characterized by difficulties in decoding words, recognizing letters and their sounds, and pronouncing and identifying words accurately. It can also make it difficult to form letters, spell, read fluently, and write. A person with dyslexia sees letters and numbers backward or reversed in order. Similar looking words are easily confused. When one student sees the word "felt," for example, a student with dyslexia might see the word "left." When another sees "dog," a student with this disability might see "god."

Because dyslexia is a hidden disorder (you can't tell if someone has it by looking at him), it can cause much embarrassment. Imagine being called on to read aloud in class if you can't tell the difference between words like "bad" and "dab" or "pots" and "post." Students with this disorder often feel incompetent and avoid writing or reading assignments. They may give up on school. But with the right support, and with the right attention paid to their special needs, students with dyslexia can succeed.

Dyslexia is only one of several learning disorders that result in special needs. Dysgraphia (a writing disability making it hard for the student to form letters, write quickly, and write legibly), dyscalculia (a mathematical disability making it unusually difficult to grasp math concepts or to perform basic math skills like addition or multiplication), and rote memory impairment (a disability making it nearly impossible to memorize facts) also prevent students who have these disorders from succeeding in classrooms that use regular teaching methods. Students diagnosed with these learning disabilities cannot learn the way other students do; their brains process information differently. It's not that they aren't as capable (in fact, many students with learning disorders have above normal intelligence), it's just that each requires a different approach to learning than the norm. These challenges result in the need for special learning environments and different teaching methods sometimes called **special education**. Students with these disorders have special needs.

Like learning disorders, emotional and psychological disorders can result in special needs, too. A student with clinical depression may not be able to carry the same workload as another student; the pressure may be too much to bear. A teenager on psychiatric medication may need to miss part of his classes to follow the dosing regimen his psychiatrist prescribes. A youth with extreme emotional disturbance may need the quiet of a smaller classroom with fewer students or may need to be schooled by teachers with special training in handling students with his issues. These students face out-of-the-ordinary challenges and require greater support and intervention. They have special needs resulting from their emotional, psychological, or learning disorders.

Not all teens with special needs have "disorders" or medical conditions. Sometimes teens end up with special needs because of choices they've made.

Fifteen-year-old Tammy knew she'd be an art instructor one day. She had it all planned. She'd finish high school and attend an out-of-state college known for its excellence in art education. She'd complete her student teaching, enroll in a graduate art program, earn her master's degree in fine arts, and then begin teaching college art classes. She knew exactly what she wanted to do with her life and how she was going to get it. She didn't count on getting pregnant.

Of course, she loved Tom. And she planned to marry him. But when Tom found out he was going to be a father, he panicked.

"It's me or the baby," he said. That was it. So much for fairy tale endings.

Tammy kept the baby because she felt it was the right thing to do. Tom dumped them both, and Tammy's dreams changed. Just getting through high school was going to be difficult. College might never happen. Tammy's future, once so certain, became a glaring unknown.

But thanks to her high school's program for teen mothers, Tammy ultimately didn't have to give up her desire to become an art instructor. She attended school right up to her baby's due date. School policy allowed her extra absences for morning sickness and doctor visits. When the baby came, the same policies allowed her to take the newborn to class with her and later, to leave him in an on-site day care center. Tammy graduated on time and, with the support of family and friends, earned her Bachelor of Fine Arts degree at a local college. She's a teacher today because her high school provided a program for teen moms.

Unlike physical or psychological issues, Tammy's special needs resulted from her choices. She chose to have unprotected sex, which resulted in her pregnancy. Still, her resulting short-term needs were no less real. For Tammy to get through high school, she required extra support and greater flexibility in her classes. She had special needs.

Other behavioral choices can result in special needs:

choosing to break the law and winding up in a juvenile detention center,

choosing to do drugs and contracting a related medical condition, including hepatitis, HIV, or drug addiction, or

choosing to run away from home and ending up homeless, in gangs, or in prostitution.

Teens in these situations need help—sometimes just to survive. They have special medical issues and schooling requirements. They, too, have special needs. As difficult as these needs may be, one other related group of special needs requires similar support: those resulting from environmental circumstances.

Nineteen-year-old Joseph is a computer science major at a community college. He works part time as a computer technician at a local car dealership where his coworkers view him as intelligent, capable, and a huge asset to the service department. The fact that he holds a job and goes to college is a major accomplishment when you consider that two short years ago, Joseph didn't know how to flush a toilet, open a can with a can opener, or turn on the light in his kitchen apartment. He couldn't even speak English.

Joseph is one of the "Lost Boys of Sudan," a group of 15,000 to 30,000 children orphaned and forced to flee their villages during the brutal Sudanese civil wars of the late 1980s and early 1990s. These children, mostly boys, many as young as three or four years old, wandered their country on foot trying to escape capture or murder by warring tribes. When all was said and done, they hiked more than 1,000 miles. More than half of the children died along the way: some starved to death; some perished from lack of water; wild animals killed a few; and others drowned when they attempted river crossings. The boys who survived tell stories of seeing enemy tribesmen slaughter their families and of crocodiles, lions, and vultures feeding on their friends. They recount months of unending hunger, thirst, sickness, and weariness. But through all these hardships, the children looked out for one another and survived.

Many "Lost Boys" (named after the orphans in Peter Pan's Neverland), found their way to refugee camps in neighboring African countries. Hundreds interviewed to come to the United States. Joseph was one of a few lucky ones chosen to begin a new life in America. Thousands remained behind.

When Joseph arrived in southeastern Pennsylvania, he knew little of how to live in his new home. He'd never known anything but wandering in the wilderness or life as a refugee. He didn't speak English, had never seen indoor plumbing, and had no knowledge of modern conveniences like electricity, microwave ovens, refrigerators, and packaged food. Joseph and other transplanted youth from Sudan needed much support and guidance to adapt to their new environment. They had special needs.

The U.S. government, the boys' sponsoring agencies, and the local school districts did much to help the Sudanese youth. They provided housing and financial assistance; they assigned mentors to help the boys shop, cook, and use the gadgets in their apartments; they offered English classes and tutors to teach them the English language; they placed the students in age-appropriate classes at local schools and offered additional learning support to help them manage their studies.

Almost miraculously, just two years later, Joseph and the other students from Sudan function like most other American teens their ages: they have jobs, drive cars, are graduating from high school, and going to college. Their needs (food, clothing, shelter, language support, schooling, etc.) have been met and will continue to be met as they transition into adulthood and independence. Their circumstances, not medical conditions or choices, caused them to develop the need for special support.

The extreme case of surviving civil war and becoming a refugee in a foreign land resulted in special needs. Other circumstances such as international adoption, placement in foster homes, extreme poverty, and child abuse or neglect can cause youth to develop special needs.

These four categories of need (medical/physical challenges, psychological or learning disorders, behavioral choices and their consequences, and environmental circumstances) result in issues that differ from the norm. Adopted children, foster children, abused children, teens in the juvenile justice system, teens with physical, medical, psychological, or learning disabilities—these kids must overcome what seem to be insurmountable challenges, sometimes just to survive.

Thankfully, in America today, most individuals with special needs can get the help they need to reach their potentials. It hasn't always been that way.

History reveals that those with special needs were rarely given protection, support, or legal status in the past. More often they were institutionalized, segregated, abused, or neglected. In some cases, they were killed or left to die. In the next chapter we look at some of the horrors people with special needs experienced long ago and how their experiences shaped laws that protect and support those with special needs today.

A PARTIAL LIST OF PHYSICAL CONDITIONS THAT CAN RESULT IN SPECIAL NEEDS

addiction

AIDS

allergies

amputation

asthma

blindness or visual impairment

cerebral palsy (CP)

chronic illness

chronic fatigue syndrome

chronic pain

Crohn's disease

cystic fibrosis (CF)

deafness or hearing impairment

epilepsy

genetic disorders

heart disorders

hemophilia

HIV

juvenile diabetes

juvenile arthritis

Lyme disease

multiple sclerosis

muscular dystrophy (MD)

paralysis

spina bifida

spinal cord injuries

stroke

traumatic brain injury (TBI)

Other life-threatening or debilitating illnesses (cancer, lupus, etc.)

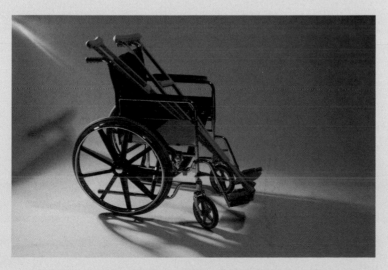

Impaired mobility is just one form of special need.

Make Connections:
Common Psychiatric Disorders in Teens

autism spectrum disorders
bipolar disorder (manic-depression)
depression
eating disorders (anorexia and bulimia)
insomnia
obsessive-compulsive disorder (OCD)
panic disorder
post-traumatic stress disorder (PTSD)
psychosis
schizophrenia
social phobias

FAMOUS PEOPLE AND THEIR DISORDERS

Fairy tale writer Hans Christian Andersen: dyslexia
Harriet Tubman, of Underground Railroad fame: epilepsy
Author Ernest Hemingway: depression
Classic composer Ludwig von Beethoven: hearing
    impairment/deafness
Impressionistic painter Claude Monet: visual impairment
Franklin Delano Roosevelt, thirty-second president of the
    United States: paralysis/polio
James Earl Jones, the voice of Star Wars' Darth Vader:
    speech impairment
Singer/songwriter Stevie Wonder: blindness
Canadian actor Michael J. Fox: Parkinson's disease
Former "Superman," actor Christopher Reeve: complete
    paralysis/spinal cord injury
British astrophysicist Stephen Hawking: ALS (Amyotrophic
    Lateral Sclerosis)

Although Harriet Tubman experienced epilepsy throughout her life, she was a leader in African Americans' fight for freedom.

Franklin Delano Roosevelt spent much of his presidency in a wheelchair. He's shown here with his dog and granddaughter.

Research Project

Find out more about one of the famous people listed in this chapter who had some sort of special challenge. Read a biography from the library on this person. How did the individual's physical challenge impact his or her life? How did he or she overcome it?

Text-Dependent Questions

1. What are some of the circumstances listed in this chapter that may cause a young person to have special needs? What four categories does the author divide all these circumstances into?
2. What "special need" did Harriet Tubman have? What is she better known for today than her "disability"?
3. What about Franklin Roosevelt? What was his handicapping condition? What did he accomplish despite it?

SPECIAL NEEDS OF YOUTH IN THE JUVENILE COURT SYSTEM

For youth who commit crimes, appropriate mental health care has been identified as their greatest special need. The Coalition for Juvenile Justice in Washington, DC, estimates that 50 to 75 percent of youth in detention and correctional facilities have diagnosable mental health or substance abuse problems, or both. Teens in these centers are more than four times more likely to commit suicide than teens in the general public. The National Mental Health Association (NMHA) agrees.

The NMHA found in 1998 that emotional or psychiatric disorders were typically not identified before the youth committed the crime. Diagnosis came after he entered the juvenile court system. Sadly, once diagnosed, most of these children received little, if any, treatment.

Never look down on anybody
unless you're helping them up.
—Jesse Jackson

Words to Understand

autism spectrum: A mental condition, present from early childhood, characterized by difficulty in communicating and forming relationships with other people and in using language and abstract concepts, which occurs in a range of severity, from low functioning to higher functioning.

autism: A psychological condition marked by withdrawal from the outside world.

segregation: The practice of removing or isolating people with differences from the rest of society.

eugenics: Science that deals with the improvement of the human race through breeding.

advocate: To push or plead for a cause.

2

A History of Discrimination: Why We Need Laws to Protect Those with Special Needs

Joyce cowered. Her stringy red hair hung over her face as she rocked in her seat, hugging her books to her chest. She wanted to melt away where no one could see her or hear her or talk to her again. *I wish they'd leave me alone!*

"Hey, Carrot Top!" one of her classmates sneered.

"What's wrong with you, retard?" another taunted.

One of the popular guys sauntered over and slid smoothly into the desk chair next to hers.

"C'mon, Joyce. Talk to us." Jerome soothed. Leaning close, he mocked, "Hey Baby, I want to hear those smooth, sweet words flowing from your lips."

The class erupted in laughter.

Morning homeroom was always the worst. For a brief time at the start of each day Joyce's teacher left her classroom unattended to monitor the halls. Joyce was at Jerome's mercy as long as her teacher was occupied in the hall.

Most days, Joyce ignored his teasing. But this time, Joyce snapped inside.

"Th . . . th . . . th . . . sthop it!" she shrieked. Her halting lisp was unmistakable. She swung around in her chair and kicked at her tormentor.

As always, Jerome was too quick for her. Her striking legs found only air. She tried to claw his face but missed. Her flailing arms spewed her books and papers all over the floor.

No! Not my books! Oh, please, not my books.

Mortified, she pushed the taunting class from her mind and knelt to gather her precious possessions. Like a desperate treasure hunter digging in sand, she clawed at the floor to sweep her books and papers together. Her tears and tangled locks spilled over the pile as she struggled to gather it all in her arms.

Where is it? Joyce thought as her eyes searched for the remaining hardcover. *Where is it? I have to find it!* With an inward sigh, she spotted her missing book. It was under the desk, two seats in front of hers.

Still leaning on her hands and knees, she reached toward the straggler. The tips of her delicate fingers had barely touched its binding when she realized she couldn't move.

She tried to lift her head, but couldn't. Something or someone held her fast. Joyce wildly scanned the floor in front of her, her eyes spying the source of her entrapment: Jerome's high-top basketball shoe was planted squarely on the ends of her long matted hair.

"Th . . . th . . . th . . . sthop it! Th . . . th . . . th . . . sthop it!" he parroted.

With a weary resignation known only to those who suffer, Joyce dropped her head and waited.

Jerome shifted, the pull on Joyce's hair relaxed, and in a split second the clumsy teen lunged for her book. She wasn't fast enough. Jerome's foot left her hair to kick the prize she sought. She watched helplessly as the treasured text spun from her reach across the tiled floor.

The class laughed again. They were always laughing. When would the torment end?

What happened to Joyce in school that morning isn't fiction. It's the true experience of a thirteen-year-old girl in a 1960s junior high classroom. During the sixties doctors and educators knew little about psychological disorders in teens. Joyce was on the **autism spectrum**, but her teachers and classmates didn't know that then. Other students thought Joyce was just strange: she was a "retard," or "oddball," or "nutcase" to them. Her teachers viewed her as eccentric, stubborn, and misbehaved.

Individuals with **autism** have serious difficulties with peer relationships: They have difficulty making eye contact, they don't pick up on verbal and nonverbal cues, they often have speech or language difficulties (may speak too loudly, too fast, or in a monotone), they may have obsessive or compulsive tendencies or may become preoccupied with certain objects (as Joyce did with books), and they can be hypersensitive to noise. Because they are often clumsy and awkward, teens with autism struggle in sports and physical education classes. Joyce was no exception, and she always ended up being the last one chosen for a gym class team. No one wanted to pick "cootie girl."

Joyce's classroom experience, however horrific, was mild compared to the treatment of people with special needs throughout history. At least in the 1960s, Joyce was able to live at home and go to school. At another time, she may not have had those options.

In ancient civilizations, Joyce would probably never have received an education. She may not have even been allowed to live. In the city-states of Athens and Sparta, citizens valued education and physical perfection above all else. Children born with disabilities of any kind were killed in a practice called infanticide. One rare exception were children born blind; early civilizations sometimes viewed the blind as possessing additional wisdom and insight because of their inability to see the world (the "blind oracle," for example). Even deaf children up to three years old could be killed. Greek philosopher Aristotle wrote "let there be a law that no deformed child shall live."

People of early Rome scorned those with disabilities. In some cases, parents of blind, deaf, or mentally challenged children drowned their disabled offspring or left them in the woods to die. If a person with a physical or mental disorder survived, wealthy Roman citizens might enslave this person for their entertainment. Joyce may have become a "jester" or "fool" to be laughed at by Roman nobility.

During the first century CE, Joyce's parents or owners (had she been a slave) may have deliberately maimed her (gouged her eyes, severed a limb, or removed her tongue) to increase Joyce's begging potential. Physically disabled beggars made more money than those with mental challenges.

Fast forward a thousand years: you might find Joyce displayed in an "idiot cage" in the town square. Idiot cages were cage-like structures, much like you see in zoos today, constructed to hold the village "idiots" (a term used to describe those with mental retardation or psychiatric disorders). Said to keep the "idiots" out of trouble, these cages often became viewing galleries and sources of amusement for townspeople and other onlookers.

If she were spared living in an idiot cage, Joyce may have been banished to a colony reserved for people considered socially unacceptable: violent criminals, prostitutes, the homeless, orphans, the poor, those with incurable diseases, addicts, cripples (as they were called then), the disfigured, the disabled, and anyone else suspiciously different from the norm. It didn't matter why they were outcasts; all "deviants" were warehoused together. Joyce would have been thrown in at random with murderers, rapists, fatherless children, lepers, and the insane. No one would protect her.

During the later Middle Ages, when most people viewed their world through religious eyes, the disabled (particularly those with intellectual or psychological conditions) were denounced as forsaken by God. Some religious leaders would have viewed Joyce as being not quite human and having no soul. Worse yet, they may have thought her to be possessed by demons and may have tried to bleed or beat the demon out of her.

With the dawn of the Reformation and other changes in religious history, Joyce's existence might have improved. Religious institutions began to see the disabled as in need of special care. Affliction was, they thought, a suffering designed by the will of God, and it was to be accepted as such. Those with disabilities were seen as "dependent" and "helpless," and in need of pity. "Good Christians" were taught that if they wanted to please God they should show mercy to the disabled and treat them with charity. Pockets of people with strong religious convictions of many faiths carried this attitude into the late nineteenth and early twentieth centuries. It was their work that later paved the way for more humane treatment of those with special needs.

Occasionally, governments tried to help. In the late 1500s, England's Parliament passed a series of laws to help the poor and disadvantaged (a category that included most people with special needs). Because of these laws, young Joyce may have been assigned to a "workhouse" and used as free labor, but her basic needs for food and shelter would have been met. This reprieve for our student with Asberger's would be short lived.

Two centuries later, Joyce would have found herself chained to a wall in a filthy dungeon, treated like an animal, and put on display again for those willing to pay an entrance fee.

By the end of the 1700s, a new and dangerous philosophy toward the disabled emerged, one that threatened their very survival. British economist Thomas Malthus published an essay advocating the killing of anyone who looked, behaved, or functioned differently than the rest of society. He argued that since the world's population was growing faster than the Earth's resources, only those who made the greatest contribution to society (those who are "normal" and healthy) should be allowed to live and use the Earth's limited supplies. Malthus and his followers would have considered Joyce "defective" and a prime candidate for elimination.

Thankfully, while Malthus pushed for the killing of disabled people in England, French physician Philippe Pinel worked to improve their lot in Paris, France. By making huge strides in scientific and medical understandings of mental illness, Dr. Pinel pushed for better treatment of his disabled patients. He ordered their chains removed, improved their hygiene and living conditions, and offered them better nutrition. Had Joyce lived in one of Dr. Pinel's institutions, she may have experienced compassionate care.

With the advancement of modern sciences in the early nineteenth century, public interest in medical abnormalities grew, and a new form of entertainment was born: "traveling museums" and "curiosity shows." "Scientific" exhibits in these shows displayed stuffed exotic animals from faraway lands, giant crystals, and laboratory jars containing deformed babies who died before, at, or shortly after birth. Next to these exhibits, people with various disabilities took center stage as "freaks" and "wonders": people with dwarfism ("midgets"); conjoined ("Siamese") twins; those born without arms, legs, hands, or feet; those with genetic disorders ("dog-faced" boys, "elephant men," "bearded" ladies, and "giants"). Physically different people could earn money by becoming exhibits in traveling circuses. In the early 1800s, Joyce may have worked as a paid entertainer in P. T. Barnum's Circus.

By the end of the nineteenth century, doctors began to identify physical and psychological differences as medical conditions needing to be cured, and the warehousing of people with differences began. "Schools," "farms," "asylums," "sanitoriums," hospitals, institutions, and "academies" sprouted up all over North America as demand grew for places to put the "impaired."

During this time period, thirteen-year-old Joyce may well have been placed in an institution, completely segregated from her family and the rest of "normal" society. Anyone considered an "idiot" or "imbecile," "feebleminded," "epileptic," "cripple," "hunchback," "deformed," "blind," "deaf," "mute," "orphan," or any one of many such labels was a candidate for confinement. People with special needs were no longer viewed as "wonders" from whom scientists could learn; they were now seen as "defective."

Institutionalizing "defective" people in the 1800s differed from when it was done during the Middle Ages. Instead of herding people of various disorders or conditions together into one place, then-modern institutions called for separate buildings or sections designated for specific conditions: the "epileptic wing," a "girls cottage" (for women only), and the "imbecile" ward, for example. Joyce would undoubtedly have been assigned to a girls cottage or placed in an asylum for "unteachable idiots." As these institutions grew and became overcrowded, Joyce may have been neglected, starved, and made to sleep on the floor.

Segregation, as described above, wasn't the worst that could happen to Joyce. The most horrific treatment of people with differences was reserved for the twentieth century.

At the start of the twentieth century some scientists believed that governments could improve the human race if they passed laws allowing only healthy, able-bodied, law-abiding people to have children. These scientists thought that if criminals, the mentally ill, or people with disabilities or medical issues reproduced, their "defective genes" would weaken the human race. Partly the result of Darwin's theories on evolution and survival of the fittest, and partly an outgrowth of a movement called *eugenics*, this belief started a chain of events that led to terrible outcomes for those with physical differences, immigrants (those who didn't speak English), convicted criminals, those with psychological disorders, and the chronically ill. New American eugenics laws barred people in these groups from entering the United States (if seeking to immigrate). Those already in the country were forbidden to marry. Some were forced to undergo a surgical procedure that prevented them from having children. With no laws to protect her in the 1920s, our thirteen-year-old Joyce would have been operated on without her consent to keep her from conceiving a child—a practice called forced sterilization. It is estimated that between the 1920s and the 1970s, more than sixty thousand people with disabilities in the United States underwent forced sterilizations.

The practices of Nazi Germany in the 1930s and 1940s illustrate the extreme result of viewing others as defective or less than human. Most people have heard of the Holocaust, concentration camps, and the slaughter of six million Jews during World War II. Perhaps less known is that the Nazi regime targeted and killed an additional six million Poles, Gypsies, Russians, and homosexuals. Even fewer realize that Hitler's killing machine warmed up on those with disabilities. Historians estimate that the Nazis exterminated (or experimented on first, then killed) from 100,000 to 250,000 disabled people in the late 1930s and early 1940s. They thought people with disabilities threatened the purity of the human race.

As a teenage girl with a psychiatric disorder, if Joyce lived in Germany during the Nazi reign, she would have been sent to a camp where she was stripped, perhaps raped, dressed in a paper gown, taken to a gas chamber, and forced to breathe hydrocyanic acid. The toxic gas would have killed her. Her body would have been dumped on a conveyor belt with several other corpses, carried into a furnace, and burned to ash. All because Joyce was a person with special needs.

When leaders of German churches spoke out against the murder of disabled children (a brave and often fatal decision by church leaders), the Nazis changed their methods. Instead of killing those with disabilities in gas chambers, they systematically starved disabled people to death, poisoned them, or made them victims of cruel, painful, often deadly experiments done in the name of "science." Some were even buried alive.

The Nazis viewed people with differences as subhuman. Their lives weren't worth living, they had no value to others, and they contributed nothing to society. Killing people with mental illness, disabilities, or physical abnormalities seemed like the perfect solution to a regime bent on weeding out weakness in the human race. Sadly, no laws prevented the Nazis from doing so.

It hadn't always been that way.

Though rare, laws to protect people with differences did exist:

> Among abusive expressions relating to the body, habits, learning, occupation, or nationalities, that of calling a deformed man by his right name, such as "the blind," "the lame," etc. . . . , shall be punished with a fine . . . If the blind, the lame, etc. . . . , are

insulted with such ironical expressions as "a man of beautiful eyes," "a man of beautiful teeth," etc. . . . , the fine shall be [a listed amount]. . . . Likewise when a person is taunted for leprosy, lunacy, impotency and the like. Abusive expressions in general, no matter whether true, false, or reverse with reference to the abused, shall be punished with fines.

Sounds fair and reasonable, doesn't it? It might even be mistaken as a law passed in recent history. In fact, this legislation is one of the earliest known recorded laws against discrimination. India's Chief Minister of Chandragupta Maurya, a man named Kautilya, passed this law in fourth century BCE! Some scholars suspect that this ruler himself was disabled.

Other ancient documents, most notably, the Hebrew Talmud, identified people with disabilities as children of God, and therefore worthy of protection. In sixteenth century England, Elizabethan Poor Laws (legislation sponsored by Queen Elizabeth) required the government to take care of those who couldn't work because of disability or disease.

These kinds of regulations gave only sporadic protection to those with special needs. With every new ruler came a new set of laws. The old laws were overruled or forgotten. Without consistent legislation or social rules to protect her, Joyce's journey through history would have been brutal at best. She would have been abused, persecuted, segregated, and discriminated against all because she had a misunderstood psychological condition. She had few, if any, rights.

Throughout history, people knew little about disabilities and what caused them. But as modern medical advancements revealed new facts about mental and physical disabilities, society began to view people with handicapping conditions differently. They were no longer seen as subhuman or a menace; they were simply people with different needs. And as people, they had basic human rights just like anyone else.

As a result of their new status, those with physical challenges and their families established organizations to ***advocate*** for and support people in specific disability groups: The League of the Physically Handicapped in 1935; The March of Dimes in 1937; The National Federation for the Blind in 1940; United Cerebral Palsy in 1949, and others. Veterans who became disabled in World War I and World War II began to receive recognition and support from the government. Athletic events for people with disabilities gained recognition, and Italy hosted the first Paralympic Games in Rome in 1960. Yes, people with differences made great strides in the twentieth century, but as we saw from Joyce's 1960s classroom experience, they still had a long way to go.

In the next three chapters we look at key laws passed during the last half of the twentieth century that dramatically improved the lives and rights of disabled persons or others with special needs. Had Joyce had the benefit of these new laws, she might never have experienced the brutality she suffered in that classroom so long ago.

Make Connections: Changing Attitudes Toward the Deaf Through Time

355 BCE	Aristotle records that people deaf from birth are "senseless and incapable of reason." Society sees them as unable to learn or be taught.
100 BCE	Elders in Athens and Rome examine children for physical perfection. If found to have birth defects, including deafness, the children are killed.
1400s CE	Dutch Scholar Rudolphus Agricola provides the first documentation that a person born deaf can learn to read and write. His writings are published a century later.
1500s	Italian physician Girolamo Cardano, whose son is hearing impaired, reads Agricola's writings and determines that the deaf are capable of reason.
1550	Benedictine Monk Pedro Ponce de Leon opens the world's first school for deaf children. Deaf children are taught to use touch and gestures to communicate.
mid-1700s	Schools are opened for the deaf in Germany, France, and England.
1817	First permanent school for the deaf in America opens. Society finally views the deaf and hearing impaired as able to be educated.

CHILD RIGHTS TODAY

In 1989, the United Nations ratified an international human rights treaty called the Convention on the Rights of the Child. It stated that *all* children (all human beings

All children have basic rights.

below the age of eighteen) are born with these basic rights:

- the right to survive;
- the right to develop to their fullest potential;
- the right to protection from harmful influences, abuse, and exploitation; and
- the right to participate fully in family, cultural, and social life.

Unlike children in many countries, children in the United States have these fundamental rights and more! The U.S. government grants its youth most rights and protections afforded in the U.S. Constitution, including freedom of religion, free speech, and certain legal protections. In addition, the Legal Information Network states that *all* children in the

Research Project

This chapter speaks briefly about the Nazis' treatment of people with disabilities. You may have known that the Nazis killed millions of Jews but not been aware that they also killed anyone they thought was "imperfect." Use the library and the Internet to discover more and write a report on what you find.

United States (including kids with special needs) also have these rights:

- the right to parental support including food, water, shelter, clothing, medical care, and an education;
- the right not to be abused or neglected;
- the right to protection by the state if abused or neglected; and
- the right to sue, although an adult must file the suit;

Children in America have far more rights than most children in the world today.

Text-Dependent Questions

1. Give some examples of how people with disabilities were treated in the past.
2. What does "institutionalize" mean within the context of this chapter? When was this approach used with people who had disabilities?
3. What did the eugenics movement lead to?

*We each have the right to learn . . . to grow . . .
to become something more tomorrow than we are today.*
—Lucie Stone

Words to Understand

attention deficit/hyperactivity disorder (ADHD): A psychological disorder marked by decreased attention span, increased distractibility, inattention to detail, impulsivity, restlessness, and difficulty with focus.

Individuals with Disabilities Education Act (IDEA): A law that provides guidelines for special education.

free appropriate public education (FAPE): Education guaranteed to all U.S. children provided by the government and according to the child's needs.

Individualized Education Plan (IEP): Education program developed for students identified as being in need of special education that is tailored to meet the student's unique needs.

least restrictive environment: Policy stating that special education students must be allowed to learn with nonspecial education students to the maximum extent possible.

due process: The right to have any law applied reasonably and with appropriate safeguards to ensure that individuals are dealt with fairly.

3

The Law Today: The Right to Appropriate Education

Eddie's kindergarten teacher, Miss Parker, was the only teacher who seemed to like the busy five-year-old. At least he thought she did. But by the end of his first school year, Eddie knew Miss Parker didn't like him anymore. Her carefully crafted note in the "Comments" section of his progress report set the tone for years of report cards to come. "Needs more self-control. Immature. Not ready for first grade." Because of her comments, Eddie repeated kindergarten.

His first grade file records his next teacher's observations: "Boys will be boys, and Edward is all boy." Months later she noted, "Edward is an active youngster who needs more discipline." The busy seven-year-old went home with sore, ruler-slapped knuckles on more than one occasion that year.

By third grade, Eddie had developed a reputation: "This student can be a troublemaker. He should be watched closely." "Needs a firm hand." "Placement in a class with strict rules and discipline is recommended."

The notes in Eddie's school files deteriorated from there: "Won't pay attention in class." "Won't remain seated." "Won't stand in line or wait his turn." "Talks at inappropriate times." "Is uncooperative." "Is careless in his work." "Constantly disrupts class." "Doesn't complete his assignments." "Written work is sloppy and poorly organized." "A poor student."

In all those years, not one of his teachers recognized the

smart, caring youth hidden beneath Eddie's behavior and poor academic performance. By the time he was seventeen, and only entering ninth grade, Eddie had had enough. He dropped out of school.

Growing up in the 1950s, Eddie lived at a time when teachers knew little about learning disabilities. They treated his behavior as a discipline problem or defiance when, in fact, his inattention, impulsiveness, and inability to sit still were the direct result of his having **attention deficit/hyperactivity disorder (ADHD)**—something he discovered as an adult nearly four decades later. He also found out he had learning disabilities.

Today, thanks to several laws enacted over the past forty years, a student like Eddie would be handled very differently:

Teachers today would test Eddie for specific learning disabilities.

They would use teaching methods that allow Eddie to use his strengths.

Because handwriting is difficult for him, today's teachers would encourage Eddie to use a computer or word processor.

If learning disabilities prevent Eddie from remembering math facts, his teachers might allow him to use a calculator.

If Eddie can't sit still, he might be permitted to take "standing breaks" at his desk, as long as he doesn't disrupt other students.

For difficult subjects, Eddie's teachers might arrange for him to participate in smaller classes with fewer students so he could receive extra help.

If disabilities make reading difficult for Eddie, his teachers might allow him to use books on tape or CDs so he can hear what he is reading.

If writing out test answers takes too long, Eddie's teacher might allow him to be tested orally (where the teacher reads the questions to Eddie, one-on-one, and Eddie answers out loud).

To help him keep track of his homework, Eddie's teachers might provide a checklist to help him organize his work.

Instead of writing book reports, Eddie might be allowed to try different ways of showing how much he knows: dramatic monologues, artwork, poetry, music, desktop publishing, posters, 3-D displays, etc.

If note-taking proves too difficult, Eddie might record his teacher's lessons on tape or be allowed to use another student's notes.

All of these interventions are standard educational practices today, and they make it possible for students with special needs, including those with learning disorders, to succeed in school. As we can tell from Eddie's experience, students with educational challenges were treated very differently forty years ago.

In the 1950s and 1960s, educational opportunities for children with disabilities of any kind (learning, physical, emotional, psychological) varied from state to state. Some states allowed students with disabilities to attend school, but kept them away from "normal" students by putting all children with disabilities—no matter what kind—together in isolated classrooms. School officials often placed students with physical disabilities in classrooms with students who had mental retardation. It was mistakenly assumed that if your arms and legs didn't work, then your brain didn't work, either. Students with physical challenges, psychological disorders, and those with retardation were lumped together in one broad category of "handicapped" students.

While educators shuffled "handicapped" kids into out-of-the-way classrooms, students with learning disabilities (of which little was known at that time) floundered in regular classes. Teachers called pupils like Eddie, who struggled with academics, the "slow" kids and often punished them or banished them to the corner to wear the dreaded "dunce" cap.

Some states wouldn't educate children with disabilities in their public schools at all. In the late 1960s, Pennsylvania's public schools denied services to children "who have not attained a mental age of five years" by the time they would normally enroll in first grade. This "mental age of five years" standard was state law, meaning that a child of any age would not be allowed to attend school in Pennsylvania unless she could perform like the average five-year-old. A ten-year-old with mild mental retardation who could read or write like a four-year-old could not go to public school. This discriminatory practice led to groundbreaking legislation in the early 1970s.

In 1971, a group of parents involved with the Pennsylvania Association for Retarded Citizens (PARC) filed a lawsuit against the Commonwealth of Pennsylvania for refusing to educate thirteen school-age children with retardation because of the "mental age of five years" law. The court decided that the Commonwealth of PA could not deny children with mental retardation access to free, public-supported education, no matter what their functional age. It also required all Pennsylvania schools to identify every child with retardation who had been previously denied an education and to place them in a "free public program of education and training appropriate to their capacity." It was the first time that a standard of appropriateness, where a child would be put into a program suited to his or her ability, was used as a guideline for placement.

Just a year later, in a similar court case called *Mills v. Board of Education*, parents of seven children with disabilities between eight and sixteen years of age sued the District of Columbia when the district refused to educate their children because of their disabilities. These seven children represented only a fraction of the students who'd been denied an education in Washington, DC: more than twelve *thousand* students with disabilities had been refused educational services in that district alone. The district claimed that they didn't have the money to give an education to students with special needs, but the court stated that the school district couldn't make children with disabilities suffer the consequences of insufficient funding any more than nondisabled children. The court ordered the District of Columbia to provide free public education to *all* children with disabilities, regardless of the extent of their disability.

These two cases became the foundation for many other lawsuits in other states. The legal decisions in these cases paved the way for a groundbreaking federal law in the mid-1970s: the Education for All Handicapped Children Act of 1975 (EAHCA; P.L. 94-142). When Congress passed this new law, more than eight million children with disabilities lived in the United States. Of that eight million, more than half were not receiving appropriate educational services, and fully one million were completely excluded from school. Something had to be done to help these children, and the EAHCA was the solution.

The original EAHCA had four main purposes:

to guarantee appropriate education for children and youth with disabilities,

to protect the rights of children and youth with disabilities (and their families),

to ensure the effectiveness of special education, and

to give federal monies to state and local governments to help them provide complete educational opportunities for all children and youth with disabilities.

Any law passed by Congress can be legally changed, and the EAHCA is no exception. Congress amended the EAHCA over several years, adding early intervention programs for preschoolers, creating transition plans for older students getting ready to graduate, changing its wording from "handicap" or "handicapped" to "disability" or "disabled," adding new categories of disability, and including assistive technology options, among other changes. These changes came through amendments to the original EAHCA and are known by the same name with varying dates: the Education of the Handicapped Act Amendments (EHA) of 1983 (P.L. 98-199); the Education of the Handicapped Act Amendments (EHA) of 1986 (P.L. 99-457); and the Education of the Handicapped Act Amendments (EHA) of 1990 (P.L. 101-476). When Congress passed the third set of amendments in 1990, they changed the name of the law from EAHCA and EHA to the *Individuals with Disabilities Education Act (IDEA)*.

The IDEA has its roots in the EAHCA of 1975 and seeks to meet many of the same goals. The amended legislation, like the original, makes it possible for states to receive money from the federal government to educate and provide services for children and youth with special needs. To receive these funds, federal law requires each state to:

1. Provide a *free appropriate public education (FAPE)* to all children and youth with disabilities, regardless of how severe their disability issues may be.
2. Base the education of a child and youth with disabilities on a complete and individual evaluation of the unique needs of that child/youth.
3. Provide an *Individualized Education Plan (IEP)* for every child found to be eligible for special education or early intervention services.
4. Educate all children and youth with disabilities in a regular education environment to the maximum extent possible. This is known as the *least restrictive environment*.
5. Provide appropriate related services (including transporta-

tion, speech therapy, occupational therapy, physical therapy, and counseling).

6. Allow parents/guardians to participate in all evaluations and decisions concerning their child.
7. Obtain permission from parents/guardians for evaluations and placements.
8. Give parents/guardians the right to challenge decisions made by the school district regarding their child's evaluation and placement (through a procedure called ***due process***).
9. Keep the child's records confidential and give information about the child to others only after the parent/guardian has provided written permission.

The IDEA strictly defines who a child with a disability can be. To qualify for services under the IDEA (to meet the "disability" requirement), the child/youth must: (a) have been assessed according to guidelines set up by the IDEA; (b) be found (through this evaluation) to have a "disability" as defined by the IDEA; *and* (c) then be found to need special education or related services because of the disability.

The IDEA defines "disability" this way:

intellectual challenges
a hearing impairment and/or deafness
a speech or language impairment
a visual impairment and/or blindness
serious emotional disturbance (includes psychological
    disorders)
an orthopedic impairment
autism
traumatic brain injury
other health impairment
specific learning disability
deaf-blindness
multiple disabilities

developmental delay (in children ages three through
nine)

The IDEA is known today as the special education law of the
United States because it tells states and school districts what they
must do to educate children and youth who require a special approach to learning. According to the U.S. Department of Education, over five million children and youth received special education
and related services in 1994 under the IDEA. Though not perfect,
this important legislation makes it possible for youth with special
needs to reach their potentials like never before.

One last piece of legislation was added to the IDEA. Called the
"No Child Left Behind Act of 2001" (P.L. 107-110), this statute
was intended to result in improvements in education for *all* children
in the United States: achieving kids; gifted kids; kids with physical
disabilities, psychological challenges, learning disorders, or discipline problems; economically disadvantaged students; racial and
ethnic minorities; immigrants; juvenile delinquents; and children
who speak English as a second language.

The U.S. Department of Education described "No Child Left
Behind" as "a promise to raise [educational] standards for all children and to help all children reach those standards." This new educational plan used four principles to fulfill its promise:

1. *The government will hold school districts accountable for
results.* Students nationwide will be tested regularly to see how
well their teachers and school districts are educating them. The
teachers' and districts' "report cards" will be made available to
parents so that parents can see how their schools compare to
others in their states. When school districts receive low marks
for their students' lack of achievement, the government requires the districts to make changes and show improvement, or
suffer the consequences.

2. *States and local schools will have greater control over government money.* According to the U.S. Department of Educa-

tion, "No Child Left Behind" gives all fifty states and every local school district within each state a greater say in how government money will be used in their districts. If a local district sees a need, that district can now use federal money to address the need without the government mandating exactly how its money must be spent.

3. *The government will encourage local schools to use methods that work.* The government will give districts money to spend on programs that have been proven to work effectively in teaching children. One program in particular, *Reading First,* and its preschool counterpart, *Early Reading First,* help children in low-income communities learn to read. The government also plans to provide training money to help teachers become better teachers.

4. *Parents and families will have more choices.* If, after its students are tested, a school receives a "bad report card" and is labeled as "needing improvement," parents of children in that school can use money from the government to pay for additional educational services: tutoring, after school programs, summer classes, and the like. If parents or guardians prefer, they can transfer the student out of the poor-performing school into a better public school or charter school at no charge. For a transfer to be allowed, the home school must be considered "in need of improvement."

The U.S. Department of Education emphasized that *all* children, regardless of age and ability, should make steady progress in school according to their potentials. In the years since the law was passed, there have been problems with it, but American educators still struggle to provide kids with disabilities with the best possible education.

Make Connections:
Your Educational Rights In A Nutshell

 The EAHCA of 1975 and IDEA of 1990 (later amended and reauthorized in 1997 as Public Law 105-17) give students with disabilities and their parents specific rights:

1. The right to a free appropriate public education (FAPE).
2. The right to ask for a special needs evaluation, at no cost to the child or parent.
3. The right to be involved in the evaluation process.
4. The right to be notified of all evaluation results.
5. The right to disagree with evaluation results and to appeal decisions made about the child based on these results. Parents also have the right to obtain an independent educational evaluation for their child.
6. The right to an Individualized Education Plan (IEP) if the evaluation determines that the child has a disability.
7. The right to obtain and use assistive technology devices and services if the child's IEP says he needs them.
8. The right to receive special education services in the least restrictive environment. By law, children with disabilities must be educated with nondisabled children to the maximum extent possible.

HOW TO READ THE NAME OF A LAW

When the U.S Congress passes an act and the U.S. president signs that act into law, the new law is given a number. That

The Statue of Liberty is a symbol for the laws that protect the rights and freedom of all who come to America.

number helps identify when the law was passed. When the Education of all Handicapped Children Act of 1975 (EAHCA) was passed and signed into law, for example, it was named "P.L. 94-142." The "P.L." stands for public law. The first set of numbers following "P.L.," in this case "94," stands for which session of Congress passed the law. In this example, "94" stands for the 94th session of the U.S. Congress. The second set of numbers (the numbers following the hyphen) indicates where in the sequence of all laws passed during that congressional session this particular law fell. In this case,

Lawyers refer to the written record of the laws Congress has passed.

Teens who are being tried for a crime will have a lawyer who represents them before a judge.

Research Project

Use the Internet to find out more about No Child Left Behind. How effective do teachers feel it is? How has it been changed or adapted under the Obama presidency? What are the problems with this law? Ask the teacher at your school what they think about the law. How do their thoughts compare to your research?

"142" means that the EAHCA was the one-hundred-forty-second law passed and signed into law during that session of Congress.

When the EAHCA is referred to as P.L. 94-142, it means that it was the one-hundred-forty-second law passed by the 94th Congress and signed into law by the president, making it a public law.

SPECIAL EDUCATION ACRONYMS AND WHAT THEY MEAN

ADHD: Attention-Deficit/Hyperactivity Disorder
BD: Behavior Disorder
CFR: Code of Federal Regulations
EAHCA: Education for All Handicapped Children Act
ED: Emotionally Disturbed
EI: Early Intervention
EMR: Educable Mentally Retarded
ESY: Extended School Year services
FAPE: Free Appropriate Public Education
FERPA: Family Educational Rights and Privacy Act
HCPA: Handicapped Children's Protection Act
IDEA: Individuals with Disabilities Education Act
IEP: Individualized Education Plan
IQ: Intelligence Quotient
LD: Learning Disabled
LRE: Least Restrictive Environment
MDE: Multidisciplinary Evaluation
MDT: Multidisciplinary Team
MR: Mentally Retarded
OT: Occupational Therapy
PT: Physical Therapy
PL 94-142: legal number assigned to the EAHCA
SED: Seriously Emotionally Disturbed

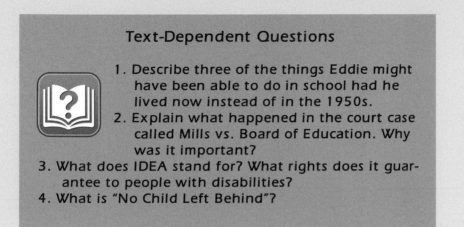

Text-Dependent Questions

1. Describe three of the things Eddie might have been able to do in school had he lived now instead of in the 1950s.
2. Explain what happened in the court case called Mills vs. Board of Education. Why was it important?
3. What does IDEA stand for? What rights does it guarantee to people with disabilities?
4. What is "No Child Left Behind"?

KIDS AND CRIME: WHAT RIGHTS APPLY?

Anyone under the age of eighteen who is accused of or arrested for a crime enters the juvenile justice system. These kids have rights, too. Beyond the right to receive an education, they have many of the same constitutional rights as adults, such as the right to due process, the right not to testify against themselves, and the right to a speedy trial. They also have the right to refuse to answer questions, to have a parent present for questioning, and to obtain a lawyer, whether or not they can afford one. Juveniles do *not* have the right to a jury trial; instead, a juvenile court judge hears the case and renders a decision.

If a minor is convicted of a crime, he will not be confined with adults (except in the rare circumstance when a child is tried and convicted as an adult). He will most likely be sent

Youth with disabilities may attend special classes designed to meet their educational needs.

to a juvenile detention center where the goal is rehabilitation, not punishment. Youth in these situations have the right to:

- be confined in safe, healthy, sanitary environments;
- be provided an appropriate education, vocational, or life skill training;
- be given appropriate medical care and mental health treatment; and
- be rehabilitated (given the opportunity to make positive changes).

There can be no truer principle than this—that every individual . . . has an equal right to the protection of the government.
—Alexander Hamilton

4

THE LAW TODAY: ACCESS TO JOBS AND PUBLIC PLACES AND SERVICES

"Mom, pleeeeease! Can I go?" thirteen-year-old Maria begged her stepmother as she held the newspaper out for her to see. "The ad says it's free, and it's only one Saturday morning. I can miss swimming just this once, can't I? C'mon, Mom. Please?"

Maria had wanted to be a model for as long as she could remember. She studied the latest teen magazines to see how models wore makeup. She borrowed videos on the art of modeling from the public library. The latest book on her nightstand, *You, Too, Can Be a Model,* was only one in a string of books she'd read recently on how to break into the industry. She had the modeling bug, and she had it bad. Now a local department store was offering a free clinic for young models. The teens who did the best in the clinic would win an additional four-session modeling course, and then, if they did well enough, would model in the store's catalogue and promotional flyers. This was her chance.

"You know how important swimming is for you," her stepmom chided. "And remember how much better your legs felt last week after your twenty-minute cool down in the hot tub. Your muscles have been so tight lately, especially with how you're growing. I really think you shouldn't miss your session."

"But, Mom." Maria pleaded. "It's my only chance. The clinic's right here in town, and it doesn't cost anything. And if I don't do this clinic, there might not be another, and then I'll never get the chance!"

"We'll see. Let's call the rehab center and see if we can get your appointment changed. Maybe they can schedule your pool time for later in the day. If they can reschedule, and *only* if they can, then you can go to the modeling clinic in the morning and PT in the afternoon."

"Really? You mean it? I can go?" Maria asked incredulously.

"Only if we can get your pool time changed," her stepmother cautioned.

After a quick phone call, Maria realized that she was finally going to taste the modeling world. The fact that Maria used a wheelchair didn't deter her. She'd seen plenty of models with disabilities in store catalogues. Saturday morning couldn't come soon enough. Little did she know how disappointing Saturday would be.

"I'm sorry, Mrs. Santiago," the modeling program's director said flatly when Maria and her stepmother arrived to register. "I can't allow your daughter to participate in today's program."

"But why?" Maria interrupted. Her face flushed when she realized that the other girls and mothers in line were looking at her.

The director ignored Maria and looked at Mrs. Santiago. "The practice ramp is set a foot off the ground. The runway is too narrow. Neither is designed to accommodate a wheelchair. Besides, I'm sure your daughter would feel out of place with *these* girls." The last comment was said just loud enough for everyone else to hear.

Maria felt invisible. It seemed like people who didn't know her always treated her this way; because she used a wheelchair they thought she must be deaf and dumb. The program director wouldn't even look at her.

It didn't matter that Maria had gotten up early, dressed in her best clothes, and done her makeup just the way her modeling tips magazine instructed. It didn't matter that her deep black hair shined with richness and beauty or that her thick flowing curls perfectly framed her dark brown eyes and flawless skin. Maria had a model's face, but the director couldn't see past her unmoving legs.

Maria didn't get to model that day in 1992. But that's not the end of her story. Though her name and other personal details have been changed, Maria is a real teenager. The woman that barred her from participating in the modeling clinic is a real department store manager. The program that Maria wanted to participate in is a real modeling program. And the events that happened that Saturday morning are a matter of public record: Maria and her stepmother filed a complaint with the U.S. government's Civil Rights Division against the major department store and its manager. Maria and her mother alleged that the store's policy of not allowing teens in wheelchairs to participate in the modeling program violated a law called the ***Americans with Disabilities Act (ADA)***. Maria and her mother were right.

Signed into law by President George Bush on July 26, 1990, the ADA made it illegal to discriminate against a person because he or she has a disability. Previous laws against discrimination existed to protect people of different races, genders, religious beliefs, and nationalities. And, as we saw in chapter 3, some laws guaranteed educational opportunities. But before 1990, no laws at the federal, state, or local levels explicitly guaranteed the civil rights of people with disabilities.

Civil rights are those rights guaranteed to all U.S. citizens by the U.S. Constitution, the Bill of Rights, and additional constitutional amendments. They include personal rights (freedom of speech, freedom to peaceably assemble, freedom to bear arms, freedom of the press, freedom from unreasonable search and seizure, and freedom of religion) and legal rights (the right to not *incriminate* yourself, the right to have a speedy trial by jury, and protection from cruel and unusual punishment). Later amendments added more civil rights: The thirteenth amendment eliminated slavery in the United States; the fifteenth and nineteenth amendments gave the right to vote to minorities and women; and the twenty-sixth amendment gave the right to vote to all people over eighteen years of age. These laws provide basic rights for all U.S. citizens.

Until the ADA became law in 1990, those with disabilities often faced great barriers to fulfilling their civil rights—especially in state and local venues. Take voting in a local election, for example: How could a woman in a wheelchair exercise her right to vote if her wheelchair couldn't fit through the polling place door? How could a blind man vote if the ballot wasn't available in Braille?

People with disabilities, as you recall from chapter 2, had a history of being treated differently: they were institutionalized, experimented on, ridiculed, neglected, or ignored. Even as society grew to accept and understand physical and psychological differences, individuals with disabilities continued to face rejection and discrimination in everyday life.

> Students with physical, psychological, or learning challenges went to school, but they were segregated from the "normal" kids.

> Restaurants who welcomed most customers turned blind people away because they used guide dogs ("no dogs allowed").

> Bus drivers refused to pick up those who used wheelchairs because the buses' narrow doors and steps made it too bothersome to help them.

> Employers wouldn't hire people with epilepsy because they didn't want an employee having a seizure on the job.

Equal access to job training, transportation, and even to local stores and shopping malls, was rarely available to those with special needs before the ADA became law.

The ADA is specific and far ranging in its legislation. It guarantees equal opportunity for people with disabilities in several areas: employment, transportation, state and local government services, public accommodations, and telecommunications. These areas fall under specific "Titles" (which is another way to identify parts of a congressional act), and each Title has its own definitions and guidelines.

⋙⋘

"HELP WANTED: Part-time driver for local deliveries. Must be eighteen or older, have valid driver's license, and be willing to work weekends. Own vehicle a plus! Apply in person at pizza shop on Market and Fifth."

Manuel read the ad a second time. This could be it! He needed a part-time job to work around his business-school courses. He was nineteen, had his license, had a clean driving record, and even had his own car. The pizza place was only two blocks from school, so it would be convenient to go straight to work from class. He decided to apply.

After filling out his application and speaking with the restaurant manager, Manuel was sure he had the job. Then his cell phone rang.

"I'm sorry, Manuel, but we can't offer you the job" the manager's voice apologized over the phone.

"But you sounded so positive when I came in for the interview. What happened?"

"Your application notes that you have a seizure disorder. Is that true?"

"Well, umm . . . yes," Manuel answered truthfully, "but my medication has kept my condition under control for a long time. I haven't had a seizure in over five years."

"That may be true, son," the manager continued, "but our

company has a blanket policy of not hiring drivers with a history of seizures. It's just too risky."

"Even when my doctor and the Department of Transportation have cleared me to drive?" the incredulous youth asked.

"Yep. It's just company policy. I'm sorry."

"But that's not fair." Manuel insisted.

"I know," The manager sympathized, "but it's just the way it is."

That may have been the way it *was*, but the pizza shop's policy would be illegal today. Employers can no longer make blanket policies that eliminate qualified people from certain positions because of specific disabilities. They can't say, as the pizza shop manager said to Manuel, "all people with seizure disorders are not eligible for driving positions." Instead, applicants must be handled on a case-by-case basis. Today, thanks to the ADA, employers would have to look at Manuel's application individually and decide how great a risk hiring him would be. In this case, Manuel met all the listed requirements for the job: he had his license, he had a clean driving record, he was nineteen, he was willing to work weekends, and he even had his own car. He'd been seizure-free for five years, and the Department of Transportation and his doctor had both said he was medically safe to drive. Today, thanks to the ADA's Title I, Manuel would in all likelihood get the job.

Title I, the Employment section of the ADA, makes it illegal for employers to discriminate against people with disabilities who are otherwise qualified to work for them. Let's say a pharmaceutical company needs a lab analyst. To qualify for the job, an applicant needs a Bachelor of Science degree in chemistry and an understanding of how to use lab analysis equipment. If a deaf applicant and a hearing applicant apply for the same job, and both hold the required college degree and experience, the company cannot choose the nondisabled applicant over the deaf applicant simply because the deaf applicant has a disability.

Employers cannot favor nondisabled people over equally qualified persons with disabilities in *any* aspect of employment: job applications, hiring practices, firing decisions, layoffs, promotions, wages, bonuses, training, benefits, advancement opportunities, tenure, leaves of absence, recruitment, advertising, and all other employee-related activities. This applies to not only jobs in private businesses but to government jobs as well.

Eighteen-year-old Scott couldn't believe it. After spending the night at a friend's downtown apartment, he discovered that his specially outfitted van was missing. It snowed the night before, and unknown to him, his friend's street was a "snow emergency route," which is a road given first priority for plowing to make way for emergency vehicles. During heavy snowfalls, the city government can declare a snow emergency, which requires all cars parked on designated snow emergency routes to be moved so that snowplows can clear the streets. Scott didn't know they'd declared a snow emergency, so he hadn't moved his van. The city must have towed it.

After seeing his empty parking space, Scott, who uses a wheelchair, made his way back to the elevator that would take him to his friend's apartment. At least his friend could drive him to the towing facility that held his van.

Imagine Scott's surprise when he discovered that the towing company's payment offices were at the top of a narrow staircase two stories up in an old office building. With no elevator, Scott couldn't get to the office to pay his fine. Since the office wasn't accessible to people who use wheelchairs, it was violating the ADA.

Title II of the ADA requires state and local governments, regardless of size, to make all departments, programs, services, buildings, and public transportation equally available to people with disabilities: Town meetings have to be held in wheelchair accessible buildings; polls and voting booths must be usable by the blind;

courts and legal services must provide sign language interpreters for the deaf. Parks and their programs, recreational leagues, public buses, and health care services also have to be physically accessible to the disabled and must include a way to communicate with people who have vision, hearing, or speech challenges.

The U.S. Department of Justice records a case in which a young man in Bridgeport, Connecticut, sued his police department under Title II because they didn't provide a sign language interpreter when he was arrested. The young man was deaf.

In another case, a county office mailed letters to all county residents about a new Neighborhood Watch program. A hearing impaired woman who received the letter had several questions and wanted to call the county offices. The letter, however, listed only standard telephone numbers to call for more information. Deaf people can't use regular telephones, but use something called a teletype machine (TTY) instead. How could the woman, who was dependent on TTY to make telephone calls, contact the county offices if they didn't provide the county TTY telephone number?

Because of Title II provisions, both the criminal suspect and the letter-receiving woman successfully challenged their local governments to provide their needed services. The police department agreed to hire an interpreter, and the county offices agreed to list their existing TTY telephone number on all correspondence.

A separate provision under Title II covers transportation. According to this part of the law, those with disabilities must be able to board and use public stations, buses, vans, railways, subways, elevated trains, trolleys, and other public transportation systems. Transit companies must install special ramps and lifts to enable wheelchair users to board trains and buses. They must allow those who use service animals to keep the animals with them on a bus or train, even when no pets are allowed. Title II requires transportation companies to make every reasonable effort to make their services available to people with disabilities.

If a person's disabilities (mental or physical) prevent him from using accessible public transportation independently, then paratransit services must be arranged or provided. A paratransit service is a transportation system that allows people who are unable to use regular public transportation to be picked up and dropped off at their destinations in special vans, taxis, or other nontraditional means.

Title II also established standards for public and private bus and van services:

New public buses have to be accessible to people with disabilities.

New private buses have to be accessible to people with disabilities.

Bus stations, including their bathrooms, telephones, water fountains, boarding ramps, platforms, service counters, etc., have to be built, rebuilt, or modified to accommodate those with disabilities.

New train cars have to be accessible to people with disabilities.

Existing trains have to provide at least one handicapped-accessible car per train.

Existing railway systems must be made accessible by 2010.

While Title II covers most ground transportation systems (trains, buses, taxis, etc.), another law establishes discrimination protection for people with disabilities who use air transportation. The Air Carrier Access Act makes it illegal for air carriers to discriminate against individuals with physical or mental impairments. Airlines must make their airport facilities usable by people with disabilities. They must also provide boarding assistance to those who need it, including people who use wheelchairs, people with medical conditions who can't walk far distances, people with vision or hearing impairments, and people with mental or psychological conditions. Airplanes must also be physically accessible to those with disabling conditions.

When Maria, our aspiring model whose story began this chapter, filed a complaint with the U.S. Civil Rights Division, she and her stepmother based their claim on provisions made by the public accommodations section of the ADA: Title III. The modeling program was a public event offered in a retail store run by a private business (it wasn't operated by the government). It was a *public accommodation.*

The ADA defines public accommodations as privately operated (nongovernment) organizations, businesses, programs, or corporations (profit or nonprofit) who own, lease, lease to, or operate facilities such as restaurants, retail stores, hotels, movie theaters, private schools, convention centers, doctors' offices, homeless shelters, transportation services, zoos, funeral homes, day care centers, and recreation facilities including sports stadiums and fitness clubs. By law, all public accommodations cannot exclude people with disabilities or provide unequal treatment.

When Maria showed up for the modeling clinic that Saturday, the director excluded her from a public accommodation, which was against the law.

Title III requires all public accommodations to remove physical barriers to participation. In Maria's case, this meant that the retail store sponsoring the modeling clinic needed to provide an access ramp to the runway and should have made the runway wide enough to handle a wheelchair. By not doing so, the store discriminated against people with disabilities who wanted to participate in the modeling program.

Thanks to Title III guidelines, all public places must be

accessible to people with disabilities. That also includes places of private treatment: pharmacies, doctors' offices, dental clinics, and hospitals. Patients cannot receive unequal treatment or unequal access to quality health care providers because they are disabled.

To make all aspects of life accessible to people with disabling conditions, telephone companies and television service providers had to get in on the act. Title IV requires all companies offering public telephone service in the United States to establish telecommunications relay services (TRS) twenty-four hours per day, seven days a week. TRS enables individuals with hearing and speech difficulties to use special equipment known as TDD and TTY. These devices enable the speech or hearing impaired to communicate over the telephone, with a screen that looks much like Instant Messaging on the Internet.

Title IV also requires all federally funded public broadcast service announcements on television to be closed captioned for the hearing impaired. When you see words scrolling across the bottom of your TV screen, as in a weather bulletin announcing a storm warning, you're seeing Title IV in action. TV broadcasts and telephone systems cannot discriminate against people with disabilities.

The ADA isn't the only legislation to mandate equal access to communication services. The Telecommunications Act of 1996 requires manufacturers of new telecommunications equipment and service providers to make their products usable by people with disabilities. Cell phones, pagers, call-waiting, call-forwarding, caller ID, third-party options, and other modern telecommunications products and services offered today must be made so that those with disabilities can use them.

Americans with disabilities have come a long way. Because of legislation like the ADA, those with physical and mental challenges—once seen and treated as outcasts—now have the right to enter all arenas of everyday life. While we've seen that this is true when it comes to obtaining education, entering buildings and buses, or using the TV and telephone lines, it is just as true when it comes to obtaining adequate health care. In the next chapter, we see that disabilities need not prevent people from getting the medical services they need. In fact, those with disabilities are making great strides in integrating the health care system.

SECTION 504: THE BASIS FOR THE ADA

Seventeen years before Congress passed the ADA, President Jimmy Carter signed a civil rights act into law that became the basis for later disability rights legislation. Called the Rehabilitation Act of 1973, this law prohibited discrimination in employment practices by any federal agency or agencies receiving federal money. In particular, one section of the Rehabilitation Act, called Section 504, stated:

> No otherwise qualified individual with a disability in the United States . . . shall, solely by reason of her or his disability, be excluded from the participation in, be denied the benefits of, or be subjected to discrimination under any program or activity receiving Federal financial assistance or under any program or activity conducted by any Executive agency or by the United States Postal Service . . .

Section 504 of the Rehabilitation Act limited its protections to individuals with disabilities in programs offered or sponsored by the U.S. government. Twenty-seven years later, the ADA broadened these protections to include state, local, and private agencies, transportation, and telecommunications. Employers on all fronts could no longer discriminate against those who are disabled.

ADA DEFINITIONS

Who is an "individual with a disability?"
    Section 504 of the Rehabilitation Act of 1973 and the ADA define an "individual with a disability" three ways: (a) a person who has a physical or mental impairment that substantially limits one or more major life activities, (b) a person who has a history or record of such an impairment, or (c) a person who is perceived by others as having such an

impairment. Unlike the IDEA, the ADA does not identify or list all specific disabilities and conditions it covers.

What does "substantially limits" mean?
Section 504 of the Rehabilitation Act of 1973 defines "substantially limits" as being unable to perform a major life activity, or significantly restricted as to the condition, manner, or duration under which a major life activity can be performed, in comparison to the average person or to most people. The ADA uses the same definition.

What is a "major life activity?"
According to Section 504 of the Rehabilitation Act of 1973, a major life activity is defined as caring for oneself, performing manual tasks, walking, seeing, hearing, speaking, breathing, learning, reading, writing, performing math calculations, and working. The ADA also uses this definition.

Ramps allow free access to public buildings for individuals in wheelchairs.

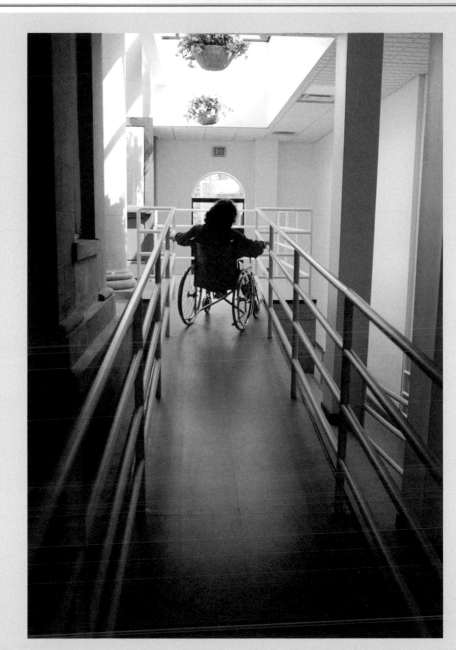

Public buildings are required by law to provide ramps and elevators for individuals with physical disabilities.

KEY FEDERAL DISABILITY LAWS

1968   The Architectural Barrier Act requires federal buildings, or buildings built or leased with federal funds, to follow federal standards for physical accessibility (wheelchair ramps, elevators, handicapped-accessible bathrooms, etc.).

1973   The Rehabilitation Act of 1973 prohibits discrimination in federally operated, funded, or sponsored agencies and programs.

1984   Voting Accessibility for the Elderly and Handicapped Act requires polling places to be accessible to people with disabilities for federal elections.

1986   The Air Carrier Access Act prohibits air carriers from

Hospitals and other public buildings provide special entrances for those with physical disabilities.

Parking spaces reserved for those with physical disabilities allow these individuals better access to stores and other public services.

Lowered curbs allow individuals in wheelchairs to navigate crosswalks.

discriminating against people with disabilities who are otherwise able to use air transportation.

1988   The Fair Housing Act prohibits housing discrimination on the basis of race, color, religion, sex, disability, family status, and national origin.

1990   The Americans with Disabilities Act prohibits discrimination against people with disabilities in employment, state and local government activities, public places, commercial facilities, transportation, and telecommunications.

1998   Section 508 of the Rehabilitation Act of 1973 (amended) requires all federal information technology, including web sites, to be universally accessible.

COMMON WAYS TO MAKE
PUBLIC PLACES ACCESSIBLE

Ramps, escalators, and elevators provide alternatives for people who can't use stairs.

Wider-than-usual doorframes allow wheelchairs to fit through.

Wall switches hung lower on a wall allow a person in a wheelchair to reach the switch.

Wider bathroom stall doors made to swing outward enable

Signs point the way to handicapped-accessible routes.

This public telephone provides a special keyboard for users who are deaf or hard of hearing.

a person in a wheelchair to enter the stall and close the door behind her.

Bathroom sinks without pipes or cabinets beneath allow a person in a wheelchair to maneuver the wheelchair close enough to use the sink.

Automated water faucets and lever handles allow those with hand weakness or dexterity problems to turn water on and off.

Braille numbers on keypads allow the blind to use public telephones and ATM machines.

Automated lifts allow wheelchair users to board buses and trains.

Removable seats in movie theaters allow room to park a wheelchair.

Extra wide handicapped parking spaces provide enough space to park and operate a lift.

Handicapped parking spaces close to building entrances allow those with mobility issues or heart or respiratory problems to walk to and enter buildings independently.

Research Project

Look around your school and community, and notice all the ways that public places are accessible to people with disabilities. Make a list. Do you see any places you think should be more accessible? Who could you tell?

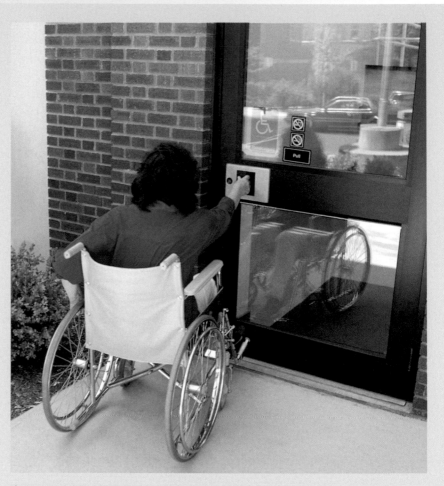

An automated door opens at the touch of a finger, allowing better access for individuals in wheelchairs.

FIVE COMMON MYTHS ABOUT ADA REQUIREMENTS AND PROTECTIONS

MYTH #1: The ADA requires restaurants to provide menus in Braille.

FACT: Waiters can read menus to customers who are blind.

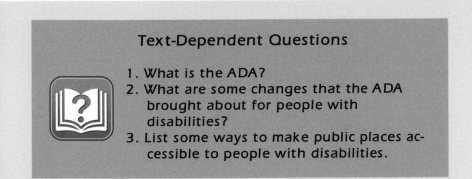

Text-Dependent Questions

1. What is the ADA?
2. What are some changes that the ADA brought about for people with disabilities?
3. List some ways to make public places accessible to people with disabilities.

MYTH #2: The ADA requires that sign language interpreters be provided everywhere.

FACT: In many situations, written materials or note writing can be used to communicate with people who are deaf.

MYTH #3: The ADA protects people who are overweight.

FACT: Being severely overweight alone is not considered a protected disability.

MYTH #4: The ADA forces businesses to hire unqualified people.

FACT: The ADA won't allow a person to claim employment discrimination if he or she is not qualified for a job, regardless of disability status. Employers have the right to hire only those people who can fulfill the job description (with reasonable accommodations) and meet all job qualifications.

MYTH #5: The ADA views guide dogs as the only qualified service animals for people with disabilities.

FACT: The ADA defines a service animal as any guide dog, signal dog, or other animal trained to provide assistance to an individual with a disability.

We are all children of one and the same
God and, therefore, absolutely equal.
—Mohandas Gandhi

Words to Understand

Medicare: The U.S. government's primary health insurance program for senior citizens.
Medicaid: The U.S. government's primary health assistance program for those with low incomes.
Supplemental Security Income (SSI): A Social Security program that provides money to disabled children under eighteen years of age who have limited incomes or come from families with limited incomes.

5

THE LAW TODAY:
THE RIGHT TO APPROPRIATE
MEDICAL CARE

"I want a life. I just want a life. Like anyone else. Just like your life. Or anyone else's life."

These words, punctuated by the hissing of a ventilator between each phrase, were broadcast in an interview on National Public Radio (NPR) in February 2003. The person who spoke them was a young man named Nick Dupree.

As a student attending Spring Hill College in Mobile, Alabama, Nick had dreams and interests similar to those of other young people his age: He enjoyed working on a computer, using the Internet, operating a Web site, and corresponding by e-mail with people all over the United States; he wanted to finish college and earn a professional writing degree with a minor in communication arts. He hoped to get a job as a newspaper journalist after graduation. But, unlike many of his peers, he most wanted to stay home. Yes, home.

Nick has a rare form of muscular dystrophy. He can't move his arms; he can't move his legs; he cannot eat or breathe on his own. A ventilator helps him take each breath, and he uses what remaining function he has in one thumb and index finger to operate a motorized wheelchair. He requires around-the-clock care.

Sixteen hours a day of skilled nursing support, plus the help his mother and grandmother provide for the other eight hours a day, allow Nick to live at home and attend school despite his disabilities.

Special laws enacted in 1965 make funds available to pay for home care and skilled nursing services for children and youth with severe disabilities. Under this law, the government would pay for up to sixteen hours per day of skilled nursing in Nick's home, but only as long as he remained a child.

When Congress passed the laws that enabled young people like Nick to receive in-home support, it created the Early and Periodic Screening, Diagnostic, and Treatment (EPSDT) program. The EPSDT program requires every state in the United States to provide all necessary medical treatment for minors who meet the eligibility requirements (usually lower income and disability diagnosis). When Congress created this program, it intended to provide health care for children—not adults—so it set an upper age limit: only those under twenty-one years of age could receive these services.

Children don't stay children forever, however, and unfortunately for Nick, the age limit meant that on the day of his twenty-first birthday, the government would stop his services. The state of Alabama wouldn't pay for his in-home care anymore since it required adults with needs like Nick's to get these services in health care institutions instead. If Nick lived in another state, he might have been able to stay at home (each state has its own rules), but Alabama's program allows only twelve hours *per week* of in-home care for adults—far less than Nick received as a youth and far less than he needed to stay alive.

According to existing Alabama law, Nick's only options were for his family to take over his care twenty-four hours a day without state help, or for Nick to give up his college career and move into a nursing home. With only his mother (who is single) and grandmother available to take care of Nick, and with his younger brother also needing care (he, too, is severely disabled by the same rare disease), Nick's family could not adequately care for him alone. But a nursing home wouldn't work either. As Nick describes in an article on his Web site, www.nickscrusade.com, living in a nursing home could be deadly:

For medically fragile individuals, going unattended for an extended period of time is not only dangerous, but possibly fatal. For someone like me on life support, for example, you need 24/7 supervision to make sure that if your air tube comes off, someone will be there to put you back on. In nursing homes, constant supervision cannot be provided because often there's one nurse to twenty or more patients. . . . Institutions are a dangerous place to be, especially for someone with my level of need.

Even if Nick could find an institution with enough nursing staff and attention, the nearest facility equipped to deal with Nick's medical conditions was two states away. To move there, he'd have to leave his home, school, and family. With no suitable options left, Nick devised a plan. If existing laws didn't give him what he needed, he would change the laws.

In March 2001, just weeks after his nineteenth birthday, this determined young man launched a campaign called "Nick's Crusade." With his twenty-first birthday coming fast, Nick knew he had only two short years to get current laws changed or he would lose his in-home care. In an article posted on-line at the iCan News Service (www.ican.com), Nick describes how his campaign started and what happened next:

On March 13, 2001, I launched Nick's Crusade . . . I knew [the law] didn't have to be this way and set out to single-handedly change it. I was able to get a bill introduced in the Alabama State Senate in early 2002 to simply force [them] to continue the care people had before age 21, after 21. "The Adult Private Duty Nursing Expansion Act," aka "The Nick Dupree Adult Care Act," sailed through committee but was stalled by . . . opposition and false rumors about cost.

The bill finally had to be withdrawn in April 2002 as it stood no chance of passage. Alabama's new 2003 legislative session [would] not start until March, after my [twenty-first] birthday.

Undeterred, Nick continued his campaign. Using only one finger and a computer, Nick launched a Web site describing his predicament, obtained 19,000 signatures on a petition to change the law, and wrote countless e-mails to politicians and lawmakers.

Finally, on February 10, 2003, largely because of his efforts and just thirteen days before his twenty-first birthday, the U.S. Department of Health and Human Services announced a new policy that would allow Nick to continue to receive the same level of care at home as an adult that he had had as a minor. Nick would be able to stay at home with his mother and brother, continue his college education, and receive the home nursing support he needed to stay alive. Because of this new law, the government would pay for these services. As Dupree stated in local interviews after officials announced the new policy, "It's a victory. I'm safe."

Nick may be safe, but he won't rest. In an interview with Associated Press writer Kyle Wingfield, Nick affirmed, "I plan to keep working on this the rest of my life to make sure that everyone can be safe and live in their community and not locked away in a far away nursing home."

Nick's dilemma reflects some of the strengths and weaknesses of current laws addressing medical care for those with disabilities. Yes, help is available, but who provides it, and where is it provided? Is institutionalization the only option? When do state governments pay medical costs? When does the federal government step in? Who makes the rules governing medical care for people with disabilities? Which disabilities are covered by these services? How long does coverage last? What kinds of services are provided (nursing care, equipment, medications, hospitalization, etc.)?

Unfortunately, a person's right to adequate medical care involves far too many laws, policies, and programs to be covered in this book. And the laws are constantly changing. We can, however, learn about the basic health care supports the government offers people with special needs by looking at the best known and most widely used programs.

In the year 2000, a single U.S. government service provided health benefits for over thirty-nine million seniors and disabled Americans. Another provided heath care coverage for over twenty-five million Americans with disabilities, including the blind and disadvantaged children. According to the U.S. Department of Health and Human Services (HHS) these two programs alone helped over fifty million people that year. What are these programs? **Medicare** and **Medicaid**.

Established in 1965 when President Lyndon B. Johnson signed the Social Security Act of 1965 and its Medicare and Medicaid bill into law (Title XVIII and Title XIX of the Social Security Act), these two new programs became the primary source of guaranteed medical coverage for people with disabilities. Though both help people with special needs, the two programs are quite different.

Medicare is an *insurance* program in which a person pays money into a trust fund during her working years. Then, the trust fund pays that person's medical bills when she gets older. Medicare assists people over the age of sixty-five regardless of income, helps young people with disabilities who meet eligibility requirements, and provides for people of all ages in the last stages of kidney disease. Because it is a federal program operated by the U.S. government, its policies and benefits are the same throughout the United States. No matter what state you live in, from Maine to Hawaii, Medicare provides the same coverage.

Medicaid is an *assistance* program; the government assists you by paying your medical bills using government money, and you don't have to pay the government back. It is a federal-state program run by state and local governments, and its policies and benefits vary from state to state. The help that Medicaid provides for teens with disabilities in New York might be completely different than the help it provides for teens in New Mexico. While some youth with disabilities receive Medicare, most depend on Medicaid because this program provides basic health care for children, families, and people with disabilities of all ages.

According to HHS guidelines only certain groups of people qualify for Medicaid:

> low-income families with children
> Supplemental Security Income (SSI) recipients (see the following section)
> infants born to mothers who are eligible for Medicaid
> children under age six and pregnant women whose family income is at or below 133 percent of the federal poverty level
> adoption or foster care assistance recipients
> certain Medicare recipients
> certain low-income pregnant women
> certain patients who have tuberculosis
> low-income women diagnosed with breast or cervical cancer;
> "medically needy" groups: the aged, the blind, people with disabilities, relatives of children deprived of parental support, etc.
> "categorically needy" groups: low-income children, people with disabilities who could be institutionalized but are receiving care at home, and institutionalized people with low incomes, etc.

An individual must fall into one of these categories to receive Medicaid. For HHS to agree that an individual fits into one of these groups, the person has to meet the HHS definition of the category, which is sometimes very complicated. HHS alone can determine if someone meets its definitions.

If a person meets the HHS definition and becomes eligible for

Medicaid, the government will pay for a broad range of health care needs:

in-patient hospital services
out-patient hospital services
laboratory tests
X-ray services
skilled nursing home services
physicians' services
physical therapy
hospice care
rehabilitation services

Medicaid will cover all of these services, but only if they are provided by Medicaid-approved doctors, hospitals, and other health care service providers. To receive government help, a person can't go to just any doctor: She must go only to those physicians whom Medicaid allows. Despite the limited choice, Medicaid-approved doctors and health care providers are licensed professionals who provide quality health services.

Because of programs like Medicaid and Medicare, millions of people with disabilities, low-income families, impoverished children, and the elderly now receive regular health care, when at one time they might not have been able to do so.

One more federal program assists children and youth with special needs: ***Supplemental Security Income (SSI)***. Though it is not a health care program, SSI, which is run by the Social Security Administration (SSA), pays monthly allowances to the elderly, the blind, and people with disabilities. As its name suggests, SSI supplements an individual's income: How much you receive in your SSI allowance check depends on how much you or your parents earn. If you don't make a lot of money and if you don't own very much, you are probably eligible to receive SSI.

According to the SSA handbook, *Benefits for Children with Disabilities* (SSA Publication No. 05-10026, August 2001), you can obtain SSI benefits three ways:

> Through the SSI Benefits for Children program: To receive these benefits, you must be under eighteen years of age, disabled (as the SSA defines it), and have (or come from a home with) limited income and resources.

> Through the Social Security Dependents Benefits program: You can receive these benefits if you are under eighteen years old, have one parent who has died, or are dependent on a parent who already receives help from Social Security.

> Through the Social Security Benefits for Adults Disabled since Childhood program: If you qualify for the dependents' benefits listed in the preceding paragraphs, Social Security would normally stop your allowance payments when you turned eighteen years old (or nineteen years old if you are a full-time student). If you have a disability, however, and had that disability before you turned eighteen, your benefits can continue into adulthood.

Anyone who receives SSI is automatically entitled to receive food stamps (free coupons used for buying food items at the grocery store) and Medicaid.

To obtain SSI, a person with a disability has to complete a detailed application on which he must provide financial information (bank records, tax returns, income history) and medical records. The information in this application allows the SSA to be sure that a person applying for SSI really needs financial help and is truly disabled. It usually takes several months to review an application, and

SSI payments don't begin until the SSA completes its review and approves the application.

In some cases, a child or youth can begin receiving payments before the SSA approves an application, but only in cases of severe disability. The law allows special provisions for children and youth with conditions so severe that the child is automatically assumed to be disabled. The SSA lists several conditions that qualify for immediate SSI payments:

HIV infection
total blindness
total deafness (not all cases)
cerebral palsy (not all cases)
muscular dystrophy (depends on severity and progression of
    the disease)
Down syndrome
intellectual disability
diabetes requiring amputation of one foot
amputation of two limbs
amputation of one leg at the hip

Children or youth with these challenges (and others not listed) can receive money from the SSA through SSI while their applications are under review. If, after review, the SSA decides the child's or youth's disability isn't severe enough to qualify him for SSI, the money SSI paid during the review process doesn't have to be repaid.

If the SSA decides that the child or youth is disabled enough to receive SSI, the SSA refers that child for health care services under a provision called Children with Special Health Care Needs or CSHCN. States call CSHCN programs by different names. Handicapped Children's Program, Medical Services for Children with Disabilities, Children's Special Services, or Children's Health Services, are just a few (your local health department can refer you to your state's CSHCN program). Most of these programs work with local clinics, in-patient treatment clinics, hospitals, private offices, and community agencies to meet the eligible child's health care needs. Even children with special needs who are not eligible for SSI can be helped by CSHCN services.

For individuals to receive Medicare, Medicaid, SSI, or to get help through local CSHCN centers, most applicants (or their families) must have very low incomes. On the other hand, private health insurance is expensive and only available to those who earn enough income or have enough benefits to pay for it themselves. Some families fall in between: earning too much money to be eligible for Medicaid but not enough to pay for private health insurance. Until a few years ago, these families often went without any medical care.

In 1997, Congress passed another amendment to the Social Security Act creating a new program known as the State Children's Health Insurance Program (SCHIP). This program covers those children and their families who aren't poor enough to have their health needs covered by Medicaid but aren't wealthy enough to pay for private health insurance. The amendment enabled states to not only provide health insurance for these caught-in-the-middle families and their special needs kids but also to provide prescription drug coverage and mental health services. By law SCHIP (or CHIP) is available in all fifty states and in the District of Columbia.

Though we've looked at a few key programs that provide health care and other benefits for those with special needs, much more is available than is covered here. Because the laws are complicated and constantly changing, and because so many programs exist, it is impossible to explain all health care options for people with disabilities in this text.

Despite our inability to cover everything related to health care in this chapter, we can learn three important things: (a) the law gives people with special needs the right to receive adequate, appropriate medical care; (b) the government provides several ways for people with disabilities to receive that medical care; and (c) when the laws or programs don't work, they can be changed! Just ask Nick Dupree.

ADA AND MEDICAID

Just as the Americans with Disabilities Act of 1990 impacted access to public places and services, employment, transportation, and telecommunications, it also impacted health care. Title II of the ADA specifically required that medical services be provided for people with disabilities in "the most integrated setting appropriate to the needs of qualified individuals with disabilities."

Using the ADA as a reference point, the U.S. Supreme Court, in the "Olmstead Decision," ruled that putting a person with disabilities into an institution (like a nursing home) who could otherwise (with services and support) live at home in his community is a form of segregation and discrimination banned by the ADA.

The Olmstead Decision ruled that a person cannot be put into an institution because he has a physical disability, if he can live at home (with appropriate help).

A boy who is blind learns to navigate his world with the help of a white cane. In an earlier time, he might have been placed in a special institution for the blind. The Olmstead Decision ruled that such an action is a form of discrimination and segregation.

That decision required state Medicaid programs to provide health care services and long-term support to individuals with disabilities according to "the most integrated setting appropriate to their needs," regardless of age. Medicaid could no longer force people with severe disabilities into institutions because it was cheaper to care for them there; it had to make every effort to allow the disabled to live in their communities as much as their conditions allowed. This standard of care applies today.

HOW THE SSA DEFINES DISABILITY

Unlike definitions used by other government organizations, the SSA's definition of "disability" is very strict and is based

The Social Security Administration provides benefits to individuals with disabilities who are unable to work at any job.

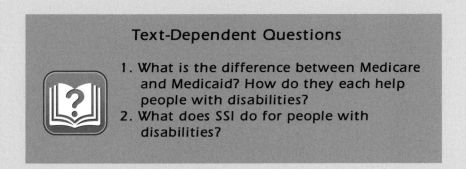

Text-Dependent Questions

1. What is the difference between Medicare and Medicaid? How do they each help people with disabilities?
2. What does SSI do for people with disabilities?

solely on a person's inability to work. Individuals can receive Social Security benefits only if their disabilities or medical conditions make it impossible for them to work at any job. They must be *completely* unable to work. The SSA does not pay or provide benefits if individuals are partially disabled or if their disabilities are expected to last less than a year.

I am always doing things I can't do—
that's how I get to do them.
—Pablo Picasso

6

NOT IN IT ALONE: REACHING POTENTIAL IN A CHANGING WORLD

A light east wind caressed Terri-Lynn Langdon's face and arms as she eased into the calm waters of Lake Erie. Oblivious to the cheers of local fisherman, well-wishers, and a band of supporters, the college honors student focused on her task; she was about to embark on the longest swim of her life.

It was 7:20 A.M., August 31, 2002. Terri-Lynn had trained for this day for two long years. The twenty-year-old athlete knew she was ready, especially after months of conditioning, but she also knew that what lay ahead would not be easy. Swimming twelve miles (19.2 km) through the great lake's seventy-four degree (23°C) waters from Sturgeon Point, New York, to Crystal Beach, Ontario, would challenge even the best of swimmers. But Terri-Lynn was no ordinary swimmer.

When Terri-Lynn was only ten months old, doctors diagnosed her with spastic diplegic cerebral palsy, a permanent condition that made her legs weak and difficult to control. Interested in swimming from a very young age, Terri-Lynn learned to rely on her arms to propel her through the water. To swim Lake Erie she'd have to depend ninety percent on her arm strokes to make it across. Her legs could only contribute ten percent to her effort. But that didn't stop the determined young Canadian who, even as a little girl, refused to allow her disabilities to keep her from pursuing her dreams. She was about to realize one of them.

Following a smooth start from the New York side of the lake, Terri-Lynn swam steadily through the morning and rest of the day. To keep up her strength, she stopped every ninety minutes or so for Gatorade, water, and a bit of fresh fruit. Then her aching arms would begin their cadence again. She swam on.

At 8:15 P.M., twelve hours and fifty-five minutes after entering the water, Terri-Lynn emerged from the opposite shore dizzy, tired, and sore, but happy. Amazingly, she averaged fifty-six to sixty strokes per minute, and though the east wind kicked up choppy waters during the last two hours of her swim, this incredible athlete maintained a pace of one mile per hour (1.5 km/hr), using essentially only her arms to pull her through the waves.

Terri-Lynn's accomplishment is one for the record books. Not only did she successfully cross Lake Erie, she raised nearly $15,000 for the Ontario Federation for Cerebral Palsy. Perhaps even more importantly, she set an astounding example of the limitless possibilities achievable by people with special needs. Terri-Lynn is not alone.

Thirteen-year-old Mattie Stepanek had six books of his poetry published. They've become national bestsellers. Diane Sawyer interviewed the young teen on *Good Morning America* where he met his hero, former President Jimmy Carter, face-to-face. Oprah Winfrey featured the poet and his books on her popular talk show, and he appeared with comedian Jerry Lewis on his annual Labor Day telethon. The Muscular Dystrophy Association (MDA) named Mattie the Maryland State Goodwill Ambassador, and later, the National Ambassador for the MDA. Mattie passed away in 2004 at the age of thirteen, which makes all of these accomplishments more impressive.

Mattie has a rare neuromuscular disease that affects his body's ability to maintain automatic functions such as breathing, heartbeat, body temperature, and digestion. One day Mattie could feel perfectly healthy and fine; the next day he could have fallen into a life-threatening coma. He used extra oxygen and needed a ventilator to help him breathe when he was tired or sleeping. He rode in a motorized wheelchair to save his energy and to carry the heavy medical equipment he needed. His condition also caused extreme physical pain.

Though small for his age, Mattie was big in heart and ambition. His three greatest wishes came true: to have his poetry published in a book, to meet President Carter, and to have his books featured on *Oprah*. He's also become a popular messenger of hope and peace not just for people with disabilities but for all people everywhere. Not bad for a kid who saw his three siblings die of the same disease, who watched his mother struggle with the same disease, and who, some days, battled just to stay alive.

Unlike Terri-Lynn and Mattie, Casey Martin didn't set out to become a disability-rights advocate. He just loved golf. Casey played sports from the time he was very young. A gifted athlete, he played them all well, but his real passion was golf. By the end of his junior golfing career, he'd won seventeen Oregon state titles and earned a scholarship to Stanford. In 1994, with teammates Notay Begay and Tiger Woods, he won the NCAA golf championship.

The up-and-coming athlete soon found himself headed for the professional golf circuit, but there was a hitch: The Professional Golf Association (PGA) didn't allow competitors to use golf carts for transportation on the course. He'd have to walk the distance—a nearly impossible task for this young man with special needs.

Casey has a rare and incurable circulatory disease called Klippel-Trenaunay-Webber Syndrome, which prevents blood from circulating properly in his right leg. The affected leg has withered and grown weaker, and Casey can no longer walk all eighteen holes of a golf course. Because of his condition, if he fractures that leg, it will not heal. Walking great distances on his weakening leg puts Casey at great risk for a fracture that could result in amputation.

Though it allows players to use carts in the early rounds of a tournament, the PGA wouldn't allow Casey to use a cart in the final rounds. Rather than give up his dream of playing professional golf, twenty-seven-year old Casey Martin filed suit in federal court in 1997. He claimed that the PGA's no-cart policy violated the ADA's antidiscrimination clause, which states, "no individual shall be discriminated against on the basis of disability in the full enjoyment of the goods, services, and facilities of any place of public accommodation." The PGA, by ADA definition, was a place of public accommodation; it couldn't discriminate against those with disabilities.

The courts ultimately sided with Casey, and he was able to participate in the Nike Tour for the next two years. He qualified for the PGA Tour in 2000 and continues to be a nationally ranked player. As Casey stated in an interview for "Faces of the ADA," an article published by the U.S. Department of Justice, he hadn't planned to become an advocate. "All I ever wanted was the chance to play and see how good I could be."

That's all most people with special needs want: the chance to be the best they can be. Terri-Lynn Langdon and Casey Martin demonstrate that it is possible to become all you hope to be and more. But it's not easy. It takes hard work, hope, determination, and perseverance. It takes recognition that all people have value and can offer something to this world. It takes identifying and pursuing your strengths and knowing your limitations. And sometimes, it takes a willingness to ask for and accept help.

When Terri-Lynn realized she had the potential to be a distance swimmer despite her cerebral palsy, she knew she couldn't train properly without someone to guide her. Like her able-bodied peers, Terri-Lynn needed help to reach her potential. So she recruited a coach. Terri-Lynn sought someone who would see her first as a swimmer—not as a person with cerebral palsy. She found that person in Vicki Keith-Munro, the most successful marathon swimmer in the sport, current holder of fourteen world records, and coach to several Canadian swim teams comprised of disabled athletes. This tremendous marathoner taught Terri-Lynn to swim farther, faster, and with more efficiency. Together, they made Terri-Lynn's lake-crossing dream come true.

Whether we have special needs or not, we all need help at some point in our lives. And there is no shame in asking. We can find the support we need if we know where to look. A local telephone book can provide lists of government agencies or legal offices that might provide the assistance we seek. An Internet search of a specific need or disability will yield hundreds of disability-specific support groups, parent groups, peer groups, and agencies targeted to people affected by the specific need. Special education departments of local schools can often provide resources addressed to specific issues. Resources exist, but we won't find them if we're too afraid or too ashamed to look or ask for them. Imagine where Terri-Lynn would be today if she'd been unwilling to ask.

Our young poet, Mattie Stepanek, could never have written his poetry books without assistive technology. Mattie relied on medical assistive technology to survive and get around: a ventilator, supplemental oxygen, a motorized wheelchair. But he also relied on assistive technology to reach his writing potential. When Mattie was yet unpublished and still dreaming that his work would be published one day, the Children's Wish Foundation presented Mattie with a computer to make his wish come true. Computers are a type of assistive technology.

HHS defines assistive technology as any device or service used to improve or maintain the mobility and independence of an individual with disabilities. Wheelchairs and stair lifts are examples of assistive technology. Word prediction software, which allows a word processor to guess complete words when only two or three letters have been typed, is a type of assistive technology. Voice dictation and recognition programs, which allow the user to speak into a microphone while the computer enters what she says, are assistive technology programs. Electric scissors for those with weak hands, talking alarm clocks that announce the time for those who can't see, and computers that "speak" typed messages for those who can't talk are all assistive technologies.

With ever-changing advancements in modern technology, those with special needs have more available to assist them than ever before. One special type of assistance comes with four legs and a collar: service animals. Mattie had one of these, too. Mattie's golden retriever, Micah, was a service dog that helped Mattie keep his balance and assisted him by retrieving objects, picking up things, and carrying his pack.

Help from assistive technology in all its forms allowed Mattie to carry his message of hope and peace to the world.

When Casey Martin wanted to play professional golf, the PGA refused to address his special needs and wouldn't listen when he objected to their decisions. Casey could not take on this powerful organization on his own; he needed the help of the law.

Let's face it. Though current laws give more rights and opportunities to people with disabilities than ever before, and though the law makes it illegal to discriminate against them, barriers still exist. Saying something is legal or illegal is one thing; getting ordinary people to accept and apply the law is another. Yes, people with differences have come a long way toward integrating all spheres of everyday life, but some parts of society still treat them with fear, misunderstanding, and rejection. That is, in part, why legislation is so important: it protects and defends those who otherwise might not have a voice. The ADA protected Casey Martin's right to equal access to a public golf tournament and allowed him to pursue his golfing potential. The same law that helped him can protect your rights and help you pursue your potential, too.

As can be seen by the many experiences recounted in this book, life with special needs can be a roller coaster ride of victories and defeats. Yet those with special needs can achieve their potentials if society gives them the opportunities granted them by law, and if they, themselves, are willing to ask for and use the help provided. But people with special needs also have a hidden advantage that often goes unnoticed: Those with special issues, *because of* their issues, often develop greater compassion, maturity, and a deeper appreciation for life than those who don't face similar challenges. This unexpected gift can strengthen those with special needs and allow them to encourage others.

In *Time for Kids*, Mattie Stepanek said, "Life is a gift. We have to make the best of it and do what we're meant to do. . . . Remember to play after every storm. We all have life storms and we need to celebrate that we get through them."

Such hopeful optimism from the mouth of a then-eleven-year-old would not have been possible without his experience of special needs. Yet that kind of message is exactly what the nonspecial-needs public needs to hear. Only those who've gone through the ups-and-downs of life with special issues can bring that kind of hope to others. The world *needs* people with special needs for that reason: it needs their message. Thanks to existing laws, advocacy organizations, and helpful technologies, people with special needs can communicate their message and achieve their potentials. The question is, will they? Will you?

QUOTE FROM TERRI-LYNN LANGDON

"Many people fail to see the potential of a person with cerebral palsy because of their disability. When I've conquered Lake Erie, I hope it will encourage people to take steps towards achieving their own dreams."

DID YOU KNOW?

Did you know that the U.S. government offers over *four hundred* programs that provide benefits for eligible citizens with special needs? The U.S. Department of Health and Human Services alone offers over one hundred of these programs, including everything from "Adoption Assistance" to "Assistance for Torture Victims" to "Scholarships for Disadvantaged Students" to "Support Services for Runaway and Homeless Youth."

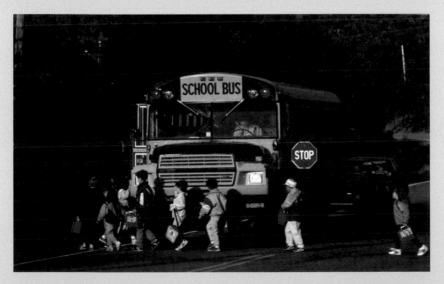

Youth with special needs are entitled to a "free and appropriate education." This means they cannot be kept from attending public schools.

Visit the official government benefits website at www.govbenefits.gov to find out what you may be eligible to receive!

HOW TO ASSERT YOUR RIGHTS

Be informed: Read newspapers and magazines for updates on special needs rights and legislation. Read about disability rights at your local library. Use the Internet to search for information on current disability issues and special needs concerns.

Be active: Get involved in your student or local government. Even if you are under eighteen years of age, you can attend town council or school board meetings. Join local special-needs advocacy groups. Write letters to your legislators. Speak up!

Be visible: Interview people with disabilities (or offer to be interviewed) for your school newsletter or local paper. Participate in public service organizations or fund-raising events. Volunteer. Get involved in your community. Ask to meet with local officials.

Be practical: Don't just complain about your situation or issue; offer well-planned, concrete steps that can be taken to reasonably address the problem.

Be patient: Changing the world can be like eating an elephant: you have to do it one tiny bite at a time.

Be persistent: Don't give up. Just as rain eventually erodes a mountaintop, long-term persistence can wear down even the staunchest resistance to change.

Children with special needs often learn in regular classrooms with support from special education teachers.

Children who are hard of hearing may use special equipment to help them learn.

FIVE WAYS TO CREATE DIGNITY WITH YOUR WORDS

1. Don't say: "John *is an epileptic*." (focuses on the disease, not the person)
   DO say: "John *has epilepsy*" or "John is a person *who has epilepsy*" instead.
2. Don't say: "Suzie struggles with cerebral palsy." (makes her condition negative)
   DO say: "Suzie is *affected by* cerebral palsy."
3. Don't say: "Dwaine *is confined to* a wheelchair" or "Dwaine is wheelchair bound."
   (assumes wheelchairs restrict those who use them when, in fact, wheelchairs provide great freedom to the mobility challenged)
   DO say: "Dwaine *uses* a wheelchair," or "Dwaine *is a wheelchair user*."

4. Don't say: "Maria is *afflicted by*" or *"suffers from* depression." (focuses on the negative and makes Maria a victim)
   DO say: "Maria *was diagnosed with* depression" or "Maria *has a depressive disorder.*"
5. Don't describe those with challenges as "crippled" or "handicapped." (focuses on inability and limitation)
   DO describe them as people "with challenges" or as "differently-abled."

Braille allows a student who is blind to read with his fingers.

Seeing Eye® dogs allow individuals who are blind or visually impaired to safely navigate busy city streets.

MONKEYS AND HORSES AND DOGS, OH MY!

Service animals are specially trained animals that assist people with disabilities in everyday activities. These animals, most commonly dogs, allow people with disabilities to be far more independent than they would be without their help. Different service animals perform different tasks, including:

- guiding the blind
- alerting people with hearing impairments to sounds
- alerting people with seizure disorders to oncoming seizures
- pulling wheelchairs
- carrying book bags and supply packs
- opening doors
- turning on light switches for those who don't have the hand strength to do so
- picking things up for those who can't bend to get them
- helping persons with mobility impairments to keep their balance

Research Project

Find out more about what it's like to have a disability. Go online and find real-life stories written by people with disabilities. What do all these stories have in common? Did a person's legal rights play a role in any of these stories—and if so, how? What did you learn from these stories that you didn't know before?

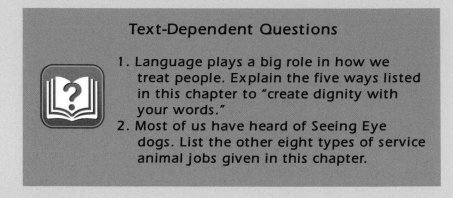

Text-Dependent Questions

1. Language plays a big role in how we treat people. Explain the five ways listed in this chapter to "create dignity with your words."
2. Most of us have heard of Seeing Eye dogs. List the other eight types of service animal jobs given in this chapter.

Most, but not all, wear a harness or collar identifying them as a service animal. These highly skilled companions are not pets but intelligent helpmates for their challenged owners. If you see one, remember that she is *working* and should not be distracted from her tasks. For more information, check out the International Association of Assistance Dog Partners online at www.iaadp.org, or other service agencies such as www.helpinghandsmonkeys.org, or www.guidehorse.org.

FURTHER READING

Crosson-Tower, Cynthia. *Understanding Child Abuse and Neglect* . Upper Saddle River, NJ: 2013.

Gale, editor. *Disabilites (Teen Rights and Freedoms)*. Farmington Hills, Mich.: Greenhaven Press, 2014.

Jacobs, Thomas A. *What Are My Rights? 95 Questions and Answers about Teens and the Law.* Minneapolis, Minn: Free Spirit Publishing, 2012.

Kaufman, Miriam. *Easy for You to Say: Q & As for Teens Living with Chronic Illness or Disability.* Buffalo, N.Y.: Firefly, 2012.

Stern, Judith, and Uzi Ben-Ami. *Many Ways to Learn: A Kid's Guide to LD.* New York: Magination Press, 2010.

FOR MORE INFORMATION

Ability OnLine (a free Internet community for children/youth with
    disabilities/illness)
www.abilityonline.org

American Academy of Child and Adolescent Psychiatry
www.aacap.org

American Association of People with Disabilities (AAPD)
www.aapd.com

American Bar Association (ABA) Center on Children and the Law
www.americanbar.org/groups/child_law.html

Americans with Disabilities Act (information and resources)
www.ada.gov

Canadian Guide Dogs for the Blind
www.guidedogs.ca

Canine Companions for Independence
www.caninecompanions.org

Dogs for the Deaf, Inc.
www.dogsforthedeaf.org

Council for Exceptional Children (CEC)
www.cec.sped.org

International Association of Assistance Dog Partners (IAADP)
www.iaadp.org

International Brain Injury Association
www.internationalbrain.org

National Alliance for the Mentally Ill
www.nami.org

National Center for Learning Disabilities
www.ncld.org

National Federation of the Blind
www.nfb.org

National Foster Parent Association (NFPA)
www.nfpainc.org

National Information Center for Children and Youth with Disabilities
www.nichcy.org/

National Resource Center for Special Needs Adoption
www.spaulding.org

Ontario Brain Injury Association
www.obia.on.ca

UCP National (United Cerebral Palsy)
www.ucp.org

Publisher's Note:

The websites listed on these pages were active at the time of publication. The publisher is not responsible for websites that have changed their address or discontinued operation since the date of publication. The publisher will review and update the websites upon each reprint.

Accessibility: An environment that allows people with disabilities to participate as much as they can.

Accommodation: A change in how a student receives instruction, without substantially changing the instructional content.

Achievement test: A standardized test that measures a student's performance in academic areas such as math, reading, and writing.

Acting out: Behavior that's inappropriate within the setting.

Adaptive behavior: The extent to which an individual is able to adjust to and apply new skills to new environments, tasks, objects, and people.

Ambulatory: Able to walk independently.

American Sign Language (ASL): A language based on gestures that is used by people who are deaf in the United States and Canada.

Americans with Disabilities Act (ADA): In 1990, Congress passed this act, which provides people who have disabilities with the same freedoms as Americans who do not have disabilities. The law addresses access to buildings and programs, as well as housing and employment.

Anxiety: An emotional state of fear, often not attached to any direct threat, which can cause sweating, increased pulse, and breathing difficulty.

Aphasia: Loss of the ability to speak.

Articulation: The ability to express oneself through sounds, words, and sentences.

Asperger syndrome: An disorder that is on the autism spectrum, which can cause problems with nonverbal learning disorder and social interactions.

Assessment: The process of collecting information about a student's learning needs through tests, observations, and interviewing the student, the family, and others. Assistive technology: Any item or piece of equipment that is used to improve the capabilities of a child with a disability.

Attention-deficit/hyperactivity Disorder (ADHD): A disorder that can cause inappropriate behavior, including poor attention skills, impulsivity, and hyperactivity.

Autism spectrum disorder: A range of disabilities that affect verbal and nonverbal communication and social interactions.

Bipolar disorder: A brain disorder that causes uncontrollable changes in moods, behaviors, thoughts, and activities.

Blind (legally): Visual acuity for distance vision of 20/200 or less in the better eye after best correction with conventional lenses; or a visual field of no greater than 20 degrees in the better eye.

Bullying: When a child faces threats, intimidation, name-calling, gossip, or physical violence.

Cerebral palsy (CP): Motor impairment caused by brain damage during birth or before birth. It can be mild to severe, does not get worse, and cannot be cured. Chronic: A condition that persists over a long period of time.

Cognitive: Having to do with remembering, reasoning, understanding, and using judgment.

Congenital: Any condition that is present at birth.

Counseling: Advice or help through talking, given by someone qualified to give such help.

Deaf: A hearing loss so severe that speech cannot be understood, even with a hearing aid, even if some sounds may still be perceived.

Developmental: Having to do with the steps or stages in growth and development of a child.

Disability: A limitation that interferes with a person's ability to walk, hear, talk, or learn.

Down syndrome: An abnormal chromosomal condition that changes the development of the body and brain, often causing intellectual disabilities.

Early intervention: Services provided to infants and toddlers ages birth to three who are at risk for or are showing signs of having a slower than usual development.

Emotional disturbance (ED): An educational term (rather than psychological) where a student's inability to build or maintain satisfactory interpersonal relationships with peers and teachers, inappropriate types of behavior or feelings, and moods of unhappiness or depression get in the way of the student being able to learn and function in a school setting.

Epilepsy: A brain disorder where the electrical signals in the brain are disrupted, causing seizures. Seizures can cause brief changes in a person's body movements, awareness, emotions, and senses (such as taste, smell, vision, or hearing).

Fine motor skills: Control of small muscles in the hands and fingers, which are needed for activities such as writing and cutting.

Gross motor skills: Control of large muscles in the arms, legs, and torso, which are needed for activities such as running and walking.

Hard-of-hearing: A hearing loss that may affect the student's educational performance.

Heredity: Traits acquired from parents.

Individualized Education Plan (IEP): A written education plan for students ages 5 to 22 with disabilities, developed by a team of professionals, (teachers, therapists, etc.) and the child's parent(s), which is reviewed and updated yearly. It contains a description of the child's level of development, learning needs, goals and objectives, and services the child will receive.

Individuals with Disabilities Education Act (IDEA): The Individuals with Disabilities Education Act (IDEA) is the nation's federal special education law that requires public schools to serve the educational needs of students with disabilities. IDEA requires that schools provide special education services to eligible students as outlined in a student's IEP, and it also provides very specific requirements to guarantee a free appropriate education for students with disabilities in the least restrictive environment.

Intervention: A planned activity to increase students' skills.

Learning disability: A general term for specific kinds of learning problems that can cause a person to have challenges learning and using certain skills, such as reading, writing, listening, speaking, reasoning, and doing math.

Least restrictive environment: The educational setting or program that provides a student with as much contact as possible with children without disabilities, while still appropriately meeting all of the child's learning and physical needs.

Mainstreaming: Providing any services, including education, for children with disabilities, in a setting with other children who do not have disabilities.

Motor: Having to do with muscular activity.

Nonambulatory: Not able to walk independently.

Occupational therapist (OT): A professional who helps individuals be able to handle meaningful activities of daily life such as self-care skills, education, recreation, work or social interaction.

Palate: The roof of the mouth.

Paraplegia: Paralysis of the legs and lower part of the body.

Partially sighted: A term formally used to indicate visual acuity of 20/70 to 20/200, but also used to describe visual impairment in which usable vision is present.

Pediatrics: The medical treatment of children.

Physical therapist (PT): A person who helps individuals improve the use of bones, muscles, joints, and/or nerves.

Prenatal: Existing or occurring prior to birth.

Quadriplegia: Paralysis affecting all four limbs.

Referral: In special education, students are referred for screening and evaluation to see if they are eligible for special education services.

Self-care skills: The ability to care for oneself; usually refers to basic habits of dressing, eating, etc.

Special Education: Specialized instruction made to fit the unique learning strengths and needs of each student with disabilities in the least restrictive environment.

Speech impaired: Communication disorder such as stuttering, impaired articulation, a language impairment, or a voice impairment, which adversely affects a child's educational performance.

Speech pathologist: A trained therapist, who provides treatment to help a person develop or improve articulation, communication skills, and oral-motor skills.

Spina bifida: A problem that happens in the first month of pregnancy when the spinal column doesn't close completely.

Standardized tests: Tests that use consistent directions, procedures, and criteria for scoring, which are often administered to many students in many schools across the country.

Stereotyping: A generalization in which individuals are falsely assigned traits they do not possess based on race, ethnicity, religion, disability, or gender.

Symptom: An observable sign of an illness or disorder.

Syndrome: A set of symptoms that occur together.

Therapy: The treatment or application of different techniques to improve specific conditions for curing or helping to live with various disorders.

Traumatic Brain Injury (TBI): Physical damage to the brain that could result in physical, behavioral, or mental changes depending on which area of the brain is injured.

Visually impaired: Any degree of vision loss that affects an individual's ability to perform the tasks of daily life, which is caused by a visual system that is not working properly or not formed correctly.

Vocational education: Educational programs that prepare students for paid or unpaid employment, or which provide additional preparation for a career that doesn't require a college degree.

INDEX

occupational therapy (OT) 10, 15, 51, 58

Olmstead Decision 98–99

Pennsylvania Association for Retarded Citizens (PARC) 48

physical therapy (PT) 10, 15, 51, 59, 93

Pinel, Philippe 34

prosthetic device 10

psychiatric disorders 11, 14, 24, 27, 37

Reading First; Early Reading First 53

Rehabilitation Act of 1973, Section 504 of 75–76

rote memory impairment 18

segregation 22, 28, 35, 38, 66, 98

service animals 70, 85, 108, 117–118

Social Security Act of 1965 88, 91

Social Security Administration (SSA) 93–95, 100–101

special education 10, 18, 44, 49–52, 54, 58, 107, 113

speech therapy 10, 15, 51

spina bifida 10, 15, 23

State Children's Health Insurance Program (SCHIP) 96

Stepanek, Mattie 104–105, 107–109

Supplemental Security Income (SSI) 86, 92–96, 101

Talmud 38

Telecommunications Act of 1996 73

telecommunications relay services (TRS) 73

teletype devices (TTY; TDD) 10, 16, 70, 73

U.S. Constitution 42, 59, 65

U.S. Department of Education 12, 52–53

U.S. Department of Health and Human Services (HHS) 91–92, 108

U.S. Department of Justice 70, 106

United Nations' Convention on the Rights of the Child (1989) 40

ABOUT THE AUTHOR
AND THE CONSULTANTS

Joan Esherick is a full-time author, freelance writer, and professional speaker who has two children with special needs. Her books include *Our Mighty Fortress: Finding Refuge in God* (Moody Press, 2002), and multiple books with Mason Crest Publishers in their PSYCHIATRIC DISORDERS: DRUGS AND PSYCHOLOGY FOR THE MIND AND BODY series and in their YOUTH WITH SPECIAL NEEDS series. Joan has contributed dozens of articles to national periodicals and speaks nationwide.

Dr. Lisa Albers is a developmental behavioral pediatrician at Children's Hospital Boston and Harvard Medical School, where her responsibilities include outpatient pediatric teaching and patient care in the Developmental Medicine Center. She currently is Director of the Adoption Program, Director of Fellowships in Developmental and Behavioral Pediatrics, and collaborates in a consultation program for community health centers. She is also the school consultant for the Walker School, a residential school for children in the state foster care system.

Dr. Carolyn Bridgemohan is an instructor in pediatrics at Harvard Medical School and is a board-certified developmental behavioral pediatrician on staff in the Developmental Medicine Center at Children's Hospital, Boston. Her clinical practice includes children and youth with autism, hearing impairment, developmental language disorders, global delays, mental retardation, and attention and learning disorders. Dr. Bridgemohan is coeditor of *Bright Futures Case Studies for Primary Care Clinicians: Child Development and Behavior*, a curriculum used nationwide in pediatric residency training programs.

Cindy Croft is the State Special Needs Director in Minnesota, coordinating Project EXCEPTIONAL MN, through Concordia University. Project EXCEPTIONAL MN is a state project that supports the inclusion of children in community settings through training, on-site consultation, and professional development. She also teaches as adjunct faculty for Concordia University, St. Paul, Minnesota. She has worked in the special needs arena for the past fifteen years.

Dr. Laurie Glader is a developmental pediatrician at Children's Hospital in Boston where she directs the Cerebral Palsy Program and is a staff pediatrician with the

Coordinated Care Services, a program designed to meet the needs of children with special health care needs. Dr. Glader also teaches regularly at Harvard Medical School. Her work with public agencies includes New England SERVE, an organization that builds connections between state health departments, health care organizations, community providers, and families. She is also the staff physician at the Cotting School, a school specializing in the education of children with a wide range of special health care needs.